Making Wooden Toys

MAKING WOODEN TOYS

ROLF SCHÜTZE

REINHOLD PUBLISHING CORPORATION
A subsidiary of Chapman-Reinhold, Inc.
NEW YORK AMSTERDAM LONDON

Printed in the United States of America
Library of Congress Catalog Card Number 66-24547

Typeset, printed, and bound by The Guinn Company Inc.
Published by Reinhold Publishing Corporation
A subsidiary of Chapman-Reinhold, Inc.
430 Park Avenue, New York, N. Y.

CONTENTS

INTRODUCTION

Rolf Schütze, renowned artisan and model maker as well as teacher of woodcraft has provided ample material in this book for the creation of simple yet charming projects. These are presented in detail so that anyone, child or adult, may successfully attempt each design with highly satisfying results.

Providing an easy introduction to woodcraft, the instructions given in each project may be followed exactly or in an extremely free interpretation which may be creatively done using the basic plans as a guide. However, once a particular project has been completed following the step-by-step instructions, most of the inherent problems are clarified so that further constructions may be accomplished in a much more artistic, knowledgeable, and freer method. As in other craftwork, stringent adherence to procedure will no longer be necessary once the forms become familiar through careful initial construction.

The rough, hand-hewn effect is maintained for its primitive charm and artistic expression and none of the pieces are polished and refined to approach the boring and overworked effect of machine tooling. This will attract young children of 8 or 9 who are anxious to use "grown-up" tools at an age when they are still too young to safely operate power tools.

Planning

The projects undertaken should be planned progressively so that the simpler toys such as the Bear and the Rooster can be made carefully at first, following the detailed plan. As facility and assurance develop with the completion of these easier projects and with further use of the tools, a freedom of expression and form will be achieved and a more uninhibited and individual treatment in construction will result.

Working Instructions

Rough pine or fir of fairly good quality is easily obtainable. The lumberyard will often have a supply of scrap pieces which are perfectly suited for these small-size toys and may be had at little expense.

A hand saw is the principal tool used, with any other available woodworking tools, an improvised work table and a vise. All saw cuts are straight and uncomplicated. The basic plan is drawn directly onto the wood block or board and may be as elaborate as the detailed instructions indicate or as simple as desired. Saw strokes should be made vertically. On a more difficult diagonal saw cut the piece can be supported at the back by some waste wood which will act as an aid in getting the saw to bite into the cut.

The more involved shapes such as the recessed front of the Pick-up Truck or the areas between the fore and back legs of some of the animals are easily formed by cutting all the way through the piece as indicated, in order to cut again where necessary, at right angles to the first cut. This simple procedure eliminates the need of a fret-saw or of hand whittling with a knife which could slip and prove dangerous to use. The various pieces are easily re-assembled with glue, nails, or brads.

Accessories

There is a great variety of adhesives available today and all have instructions for use on the labels. Clamping the glued pieces together is advantageous but is only necessary with the larger pieces.

Should any surface become soiled, the wood is renewed by sandpapering with #2 coarse sandpaper loosely folded over a block, and corners are reached by using the edge of this "tool." Too much sandpapering should be avoided to preserve the texture of the rough saw cuts on the finished toys and keep their handmade look.

Other small tools such as a metal ruler, a square, pincers, metal countersink, shears, screwdriver, awl, nail set, auger or drill with an auger bit for drilling 3/8", 1/2", 1", 1 3/8" holes will aid in working the wood.

Plywood in standard 3/8" and 1/4" width is used as is 1" and 2" wood stripping. Other woods such as mahogany, oak, and teak can be used although they are harder and more difficult to work.

Miscellaneous

Brads in various sizes and 2" 6d finishing nails are used in the assemblies. Many wood stains are available at supply stores. Plastic paint is best to use on raw wood as it dries quickly, covers very well, and is not readily absorbed.

Upholsterers' roundhead tacks make fine golden or silver "eyes" for all the animals. Metal eyelets (1/4" and 5/16") provide a smooth-working hub for wooden wheels, and leather findings, cotton, cane, pipe cleaners, bits of rope, and assorted screws should be on hand for use where needed.

Projections

The projection is a drawing of the object seen from two different sides.

Isometrics

The isometric is a three-dimensional drawing where the proportions are apparent and where all the lines are parallel.

Reading the Drawings

A two-dimensional line drawing clarifies the instructive diagram and in many cases a drawing of an entire separated assembly is included to show the position of each piece as it is to be assembled. An extra 3/4" is added to the length to allow for squaring off the block before the tracing is done.

The solid line represents the section to be cut with the saw.

The broken line - - - - is a continuation of the solid line to indicate that it should continue although it cannot be seen. This is only used in certain drawings for extra clarity.

The dot and dash . - . - . - is used to indicate areas to be discarded. In some instances it indicates a slanted surface.

Cross-hatching is only used to emphasize the planes and does not refer to a particular side of the wood.

List of Materials

Pine or fir in the following sizes:

Stock size	*Dressed size*
1″ x 2½″	¾″ x 2 ⅛″
1″ x 6″	¾″ x 5 ⅝″
1¼″ x 1¼″	1 1/16″ x 1 1/16″
1¼″ x 1½″	1 1/16″ x 1 5/16″
1¼″ x 2½″	1 1/16″ x 2 ⅛″
1¼″ x 3″	1 1/16″ x 2 ⅝″
1¼″ x 3½″	1 1/16″ x 3 ⅛″
1¼″ x 4″	1 1/16″ x 3 ⅝″
1¼″ x 5″	1 1/16″ x 4 ⅝″
1¼″ x 6″	1 1/16″ x 5 ⅝″
1¼″ x 8″	1 1/16″ x 7½″
1½″ x 6″	1 5/16″ x 5 ⅝″
2″ x 6″	1 ⅝″ x 5 ⅝″
2″ x 8″	1 ⅝″ x 7 ½″
2½″ x 2½″	2 ⅛″ x 2 ⅛″

Brad Sizes:

½″ 19 ga.; ¾″ 18 ga.; ⅞″ 17 ga.; 1¼″ 16 ga.

Screw Sizes:

Flathead — 1¼″ No. 6, 1½″ No. 6, 2″ No. 8
Roundhead — ¾″ No. 5, 1″ No. 5, ¾″ No. 6, 1″ No. 6

Projects

TRANSFERRING THE DRAWING

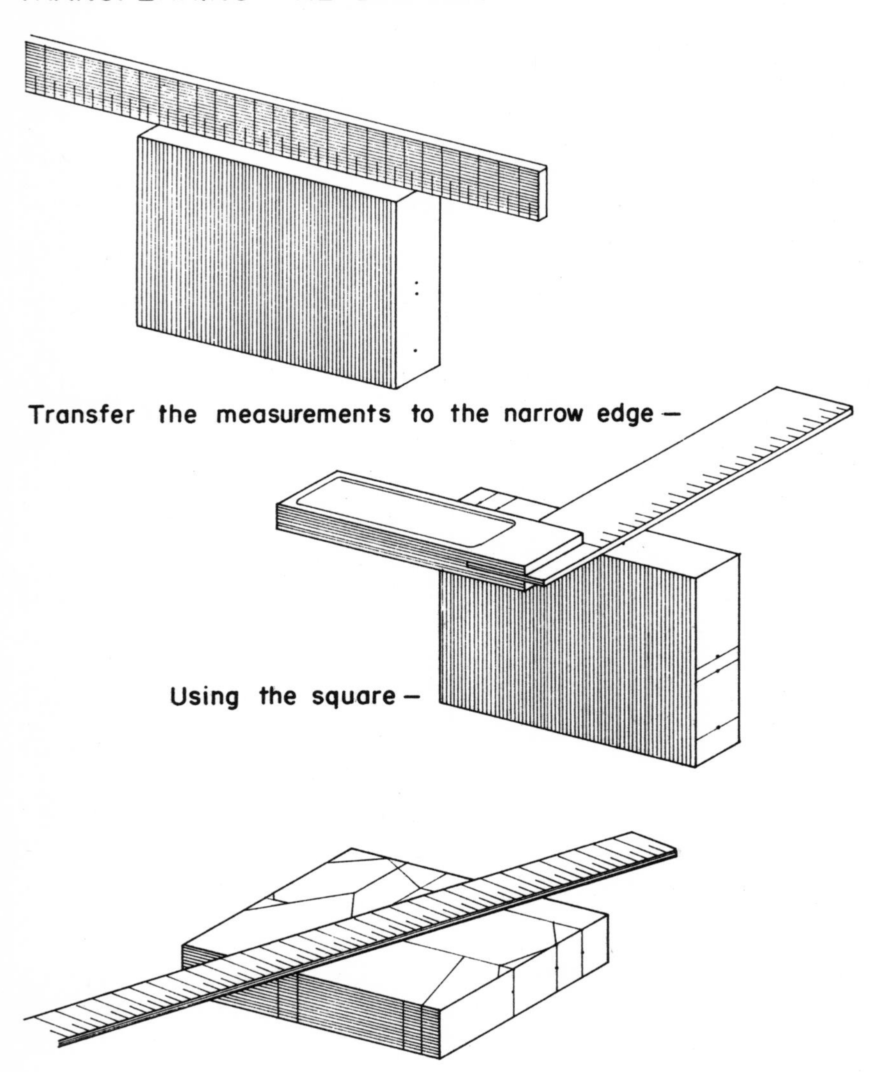

Transfer the measurements to the narrow edge –

Using the square –

Connecting the outline using a ruler.

SAWING THE DONKEY

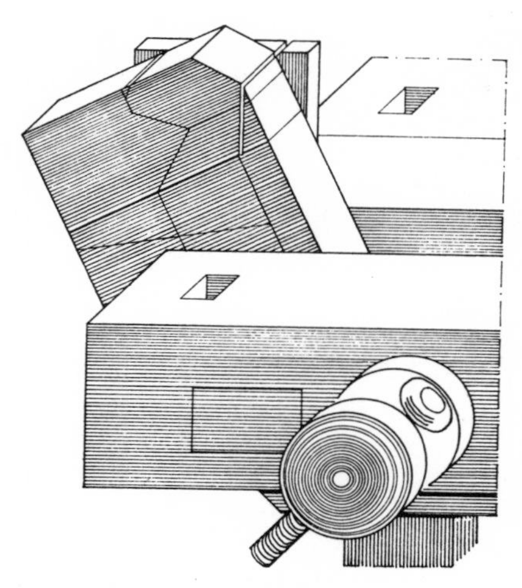

Use a supporting block of wood when sawing the neck.

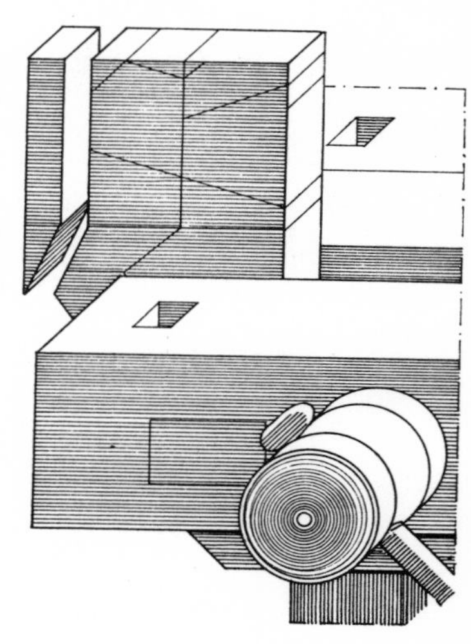

Turn and saw the back.

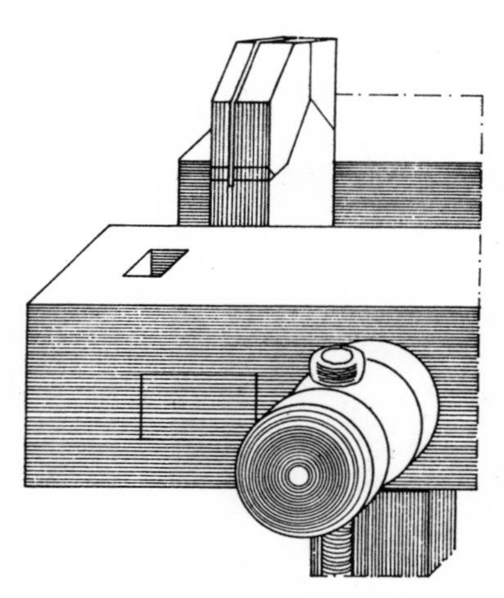

Before the head is sawed away from the wood block, slots must be cut.

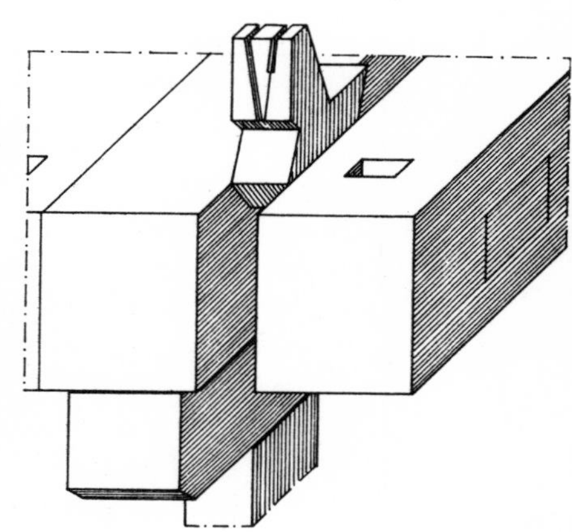

Saw out the piece between the legs.

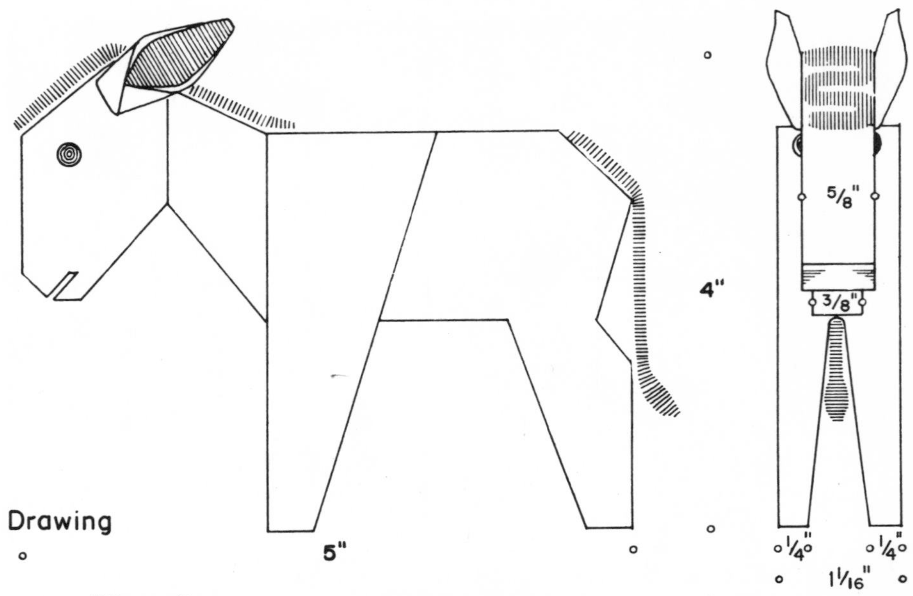

Donkey

In making the donkey the wood must be divided into two pieces, later to be rejoined with glue. The tail and mane are made of pipe cleaners, the ears of leather findings. A drawing is made for transfer to the wood.

Materials Wood: 1 1/16″ x 5″ x 4¾″ (stock 1¼″ x 6″) — trim to 5″.
2 pipe cleaners and a piece of leather 1¼″ x 2½″
2 upholsterers' nails for eyes

Procedure

Cut the wood to a length of 4″. Measure off the narrow edge. Square the piece and transfer the outline onto the broad surface using a ruler. Draw vertical and horizontal lines following diagram. (See page 12.)

Saw the outline. Begin with forehead, neck, back, and rump. To saw the neck and back use a supporting wood block. In order to saw the stomach and neck, divide the body at A and B. (See the preceding instructions on page 13.)

Before the body pieces are assembled saw out the area between the legs by boring a 3/16″ hole even with the stomach and sawing up to it.

In shaping the head the waste wood may be used for support while sawing one side of the head to thin it to ⅝″. Finish the head.

Thin the neck by sawing a depression about 1/8″ deep on each side up to line C. (See Isometric diagram.)

Saw lines for mouth and ears. The ears are made from small pieces of leather as shown in the drawing; they are glued into the saw cut or right to the side of the head, omitting the saw cut. Attach the eyes.

When the head is finished, glue it to the body.

Forelock and mane are made of pipe cleaners, bent in a tight zigzag over the forehead, and laid closely against the neck then fastened with glue. The tail is also a pipe cleaner which is glued into a hole just below the back and twisted at the end for a tassel.

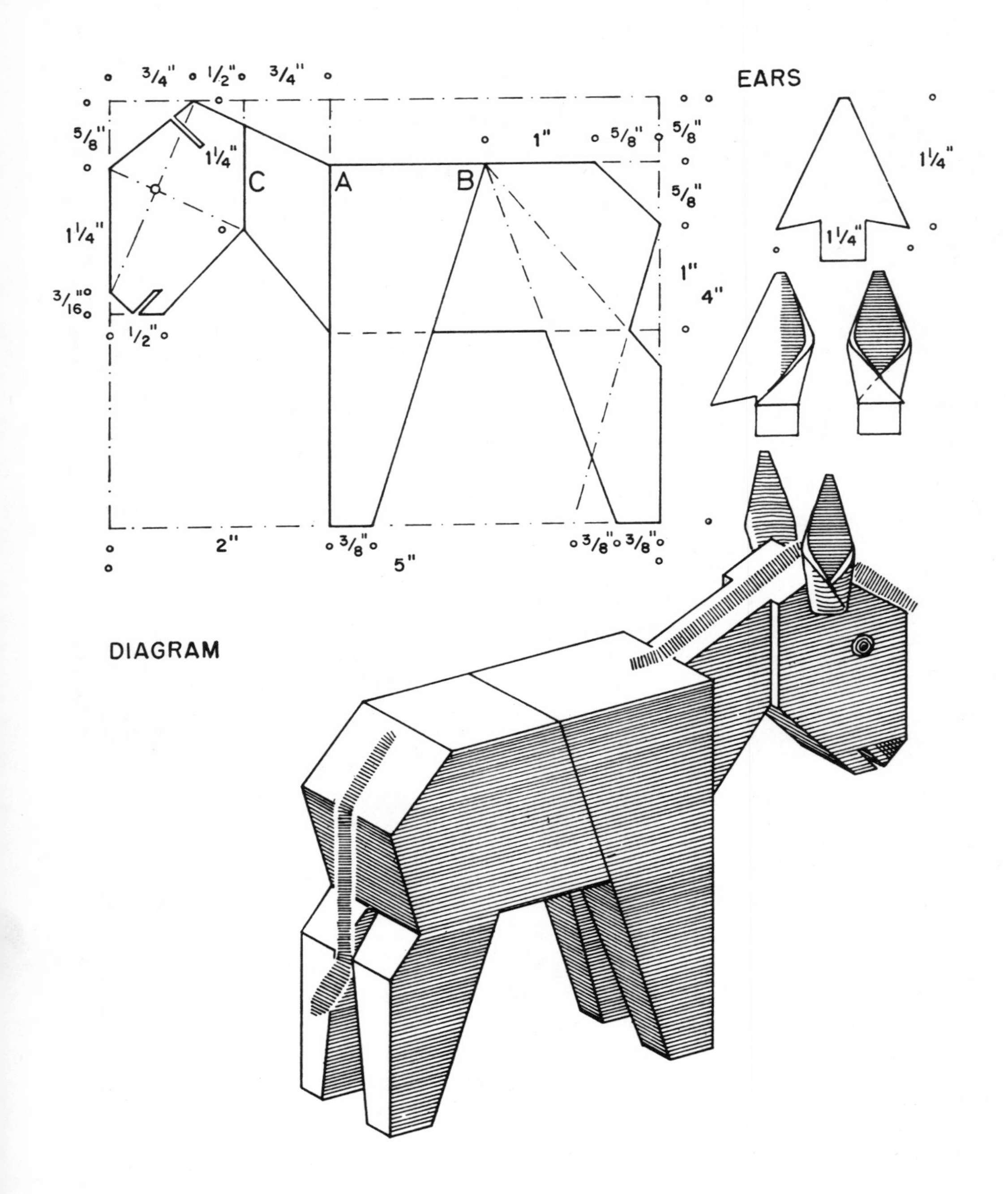
EARS
DIAGRAM
A
B
C
3/4"
1/2"
3/4"
5/8"
1 1/4"
1 1/4"
3/16"
1/2"
2"
3/8"
5"
3/8"
3/8"
1"
5/8"
5/8"
5/8"
1"
4"
1 1/4"
1 1/4"

Mountain Goat

The goat is made of three pieces which are first shaped, then glued and nailed together.

Materials Wood: 1 1/16″ x 5″ x 4¾″ (stock 1¼″ x 6″) —trim to 5″.
Brads: 1¼″ 16 ga. and 2″ 6d finishing nails. 2 nails for eyes.
Leather for ears and tail.
3/16″ cane for horns.

Procedure

Cut the wood to a height of 4″. Measure off the narrow edge, square,

MOUNTAIN
GOAT

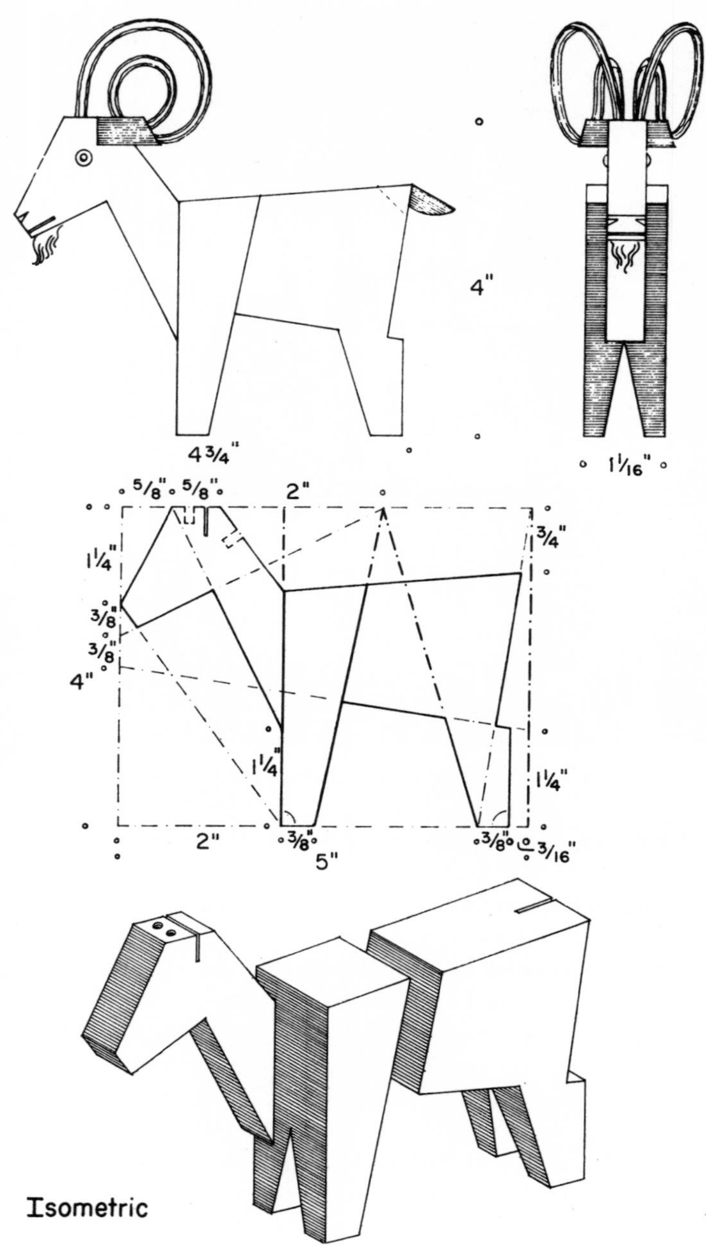

Isometric

and transfer the outline onto the broad surface using a ruler. (See drawing page 18.)

Saw outline. In order to saw the stomach and underside of the neck, divide the figure at forelegs, front, and back lines.

In shaping the head, scrap wood may be used for support while sawing away $3/8''$ from the thickness of the piece.

Saw lines for ears and tail, bore holes for inserting horns at the top of head and in the neck to prevent the twisted horns from rolling up.

Saw out the space between the legs, glue and nail the three pieces together. Set in the eyes. Cut out ears and tail and glue into saw cuts. Soften cane for horns in water, twist into shape and glue ends into precut holes.

A hole for a candle can be bored into its back and the goat may then be painted with plastic paint to make an attractive table decoration.

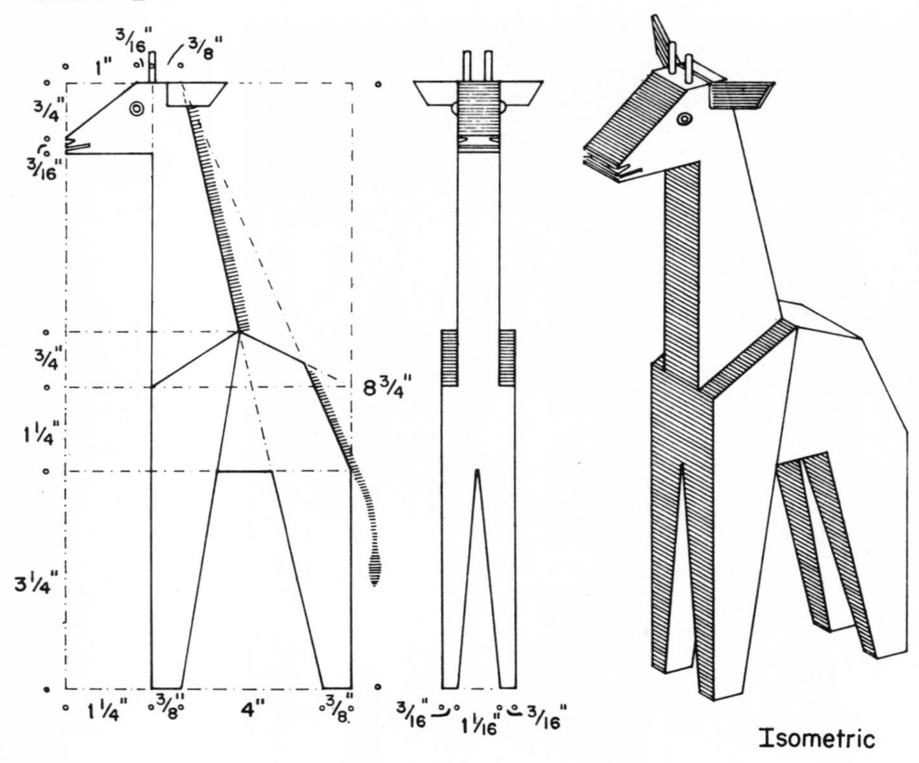

Giraffe

The figure is made of only two pieces.

Materials Wood: 1 1/16″ x 4″ x 9½″ (stock 1¼″ x 5″) —trim to 4″.
Brads: ¾″ 18 ga. Nails for eyes.
Leather for ears, cane for horns.
Pipe cleaners for mane and tail.

Procedure

Cut the wood to a height of 8¾″. Measure off the narrow edge, square, and transfer outline to the broad surface using a ruler.

Saw the figure except for the slanting back line which should be cut after the assembly is completed.

In order to saw the stomach line, divide the body behind forelegs.

To form the narrow edge of the head and neck, cut along each side so that the remaining middle piece is ⅝″ wide. Saw off these side pieces very carefully, first along the length, then crosswise.

Saw out the area between the legs, saw lines for ears, and bore holes to insert horns and tail. Glue body together and set in a clamp. When glue is dry saw the back. Then glue in horns, tail, and add mane.

Horse

The horse is made all in one piece.

Materials Wood: 1 1/16″ x 4″ x 5½″ (stock 1¼″ x 5″) —trim to 4″.
Nails for eyes.

Procedure

Cut the wood to a length of 4¾″. Measure off the narrow edge, square, and transfer outline onto the broad surface using a ruler.

Bore the hole between the legs so that as closely as possible, the lines will form a tangent to the hole.

Saw the horse figure. Begin with the front, the head (take care in making the little cut between the ears and the mane), the mane, etc.

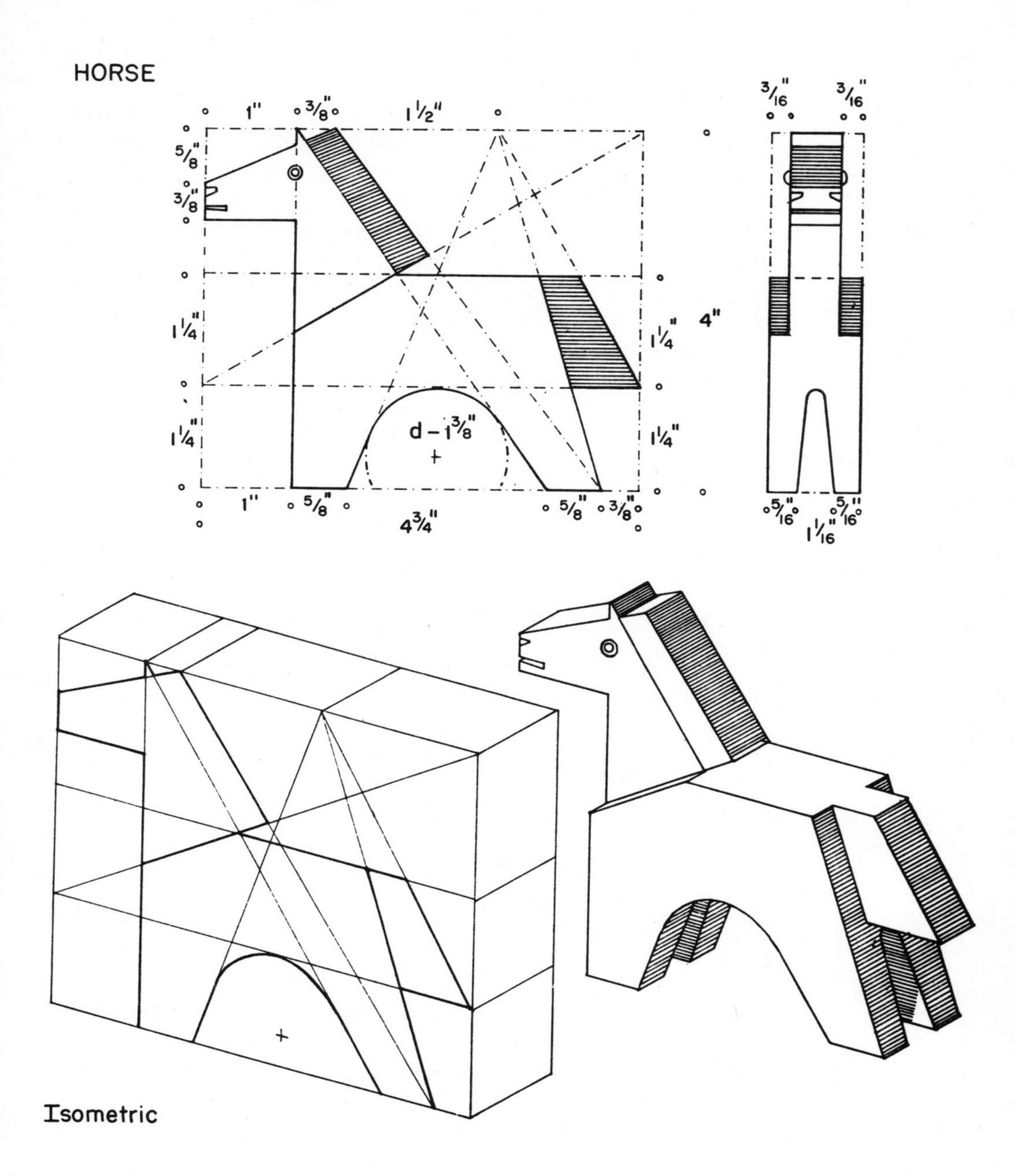
HORSE
1"
3/8"
1 1/2"
5/8"
3/8"
1 1/4"
1 1/4"
4"
1 1/4"
1 1/4"
d - 1 3/8"
1"
5/8"
4 3/4"
5/8"
3/8"
3/16"
3/16"
5/16"
5/16"
1 1/16"
Isometric

To make the narrow parts of the head, neck, and tail cut along each side so that the remaining middle piece is 5/8″ wide. Saw off these side pieces very carefully, first along the length, then crosswise.

Separate the legs by making two lengthwise saw cuts near the prebored hole. The waste wood can be removed with a small chisel.

The horse may be painted with plastic paint, coloring the mane and tail black. The eyes can then be added.

Horse Cart

The cart is intended to go with the horse shown on the opposite page. It is made from 3/8″ wood in the form of a little box, with a stationary axle and movable wheels.

Materials Wood: 3/8″ x 4″ x 12¾″ (stock 5″ wide) —trim to 4″.
3/16″ plywood for four 1¼″ wheels.
Screws: ¾″ No. 6 roundhead.
Brads: ¾″ 18 ga. Small tacks.
Eyelets and small washers for wheel hubs.

Procedure

Trim wood to 12″ length and trace according to layout on page 26. There will be about ¼″ scrap on each edge.

Cut out individual pieces. The side pieces must be cut lengthwise to half-thickness to form the two sides before it is sawed away from the end pieces which fit between them in the finished cart.

Make the shafts by sawing one shaft completely away so that the waste wood can be removed: The piece can then be glued and nailed back into place to finish the shaft.

HORSE CART

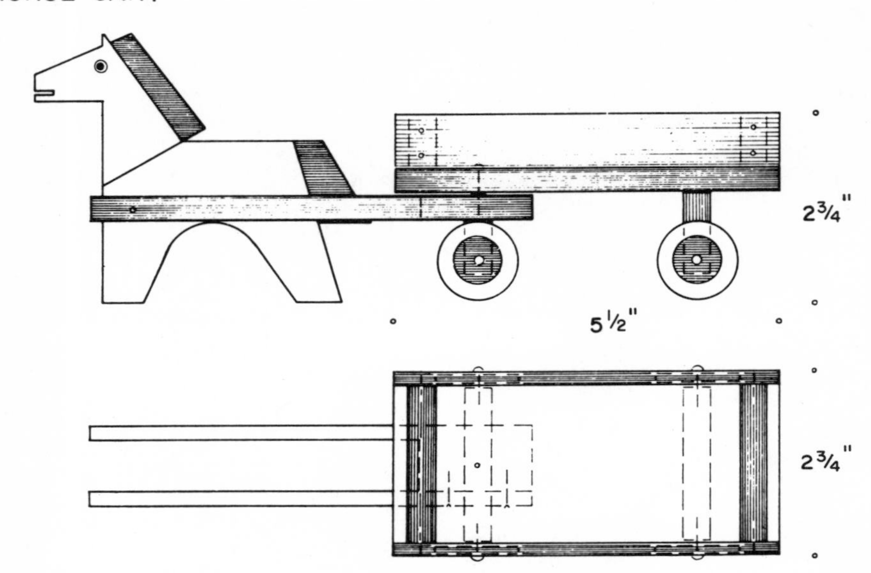

Sawing Layout

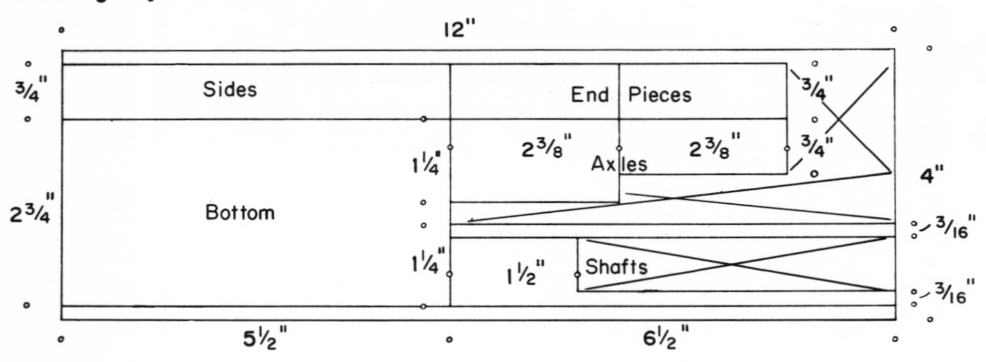

Assemble the cart by first putting the frame together and fastening the bottom with tacks. Fasten the front axle to the shafts and set it onto the cart with a roundhead screw and washer.

Bore throuh wheels and set eyelets in place. Attach wheels to axles.

Paint cart.

ROOSTER

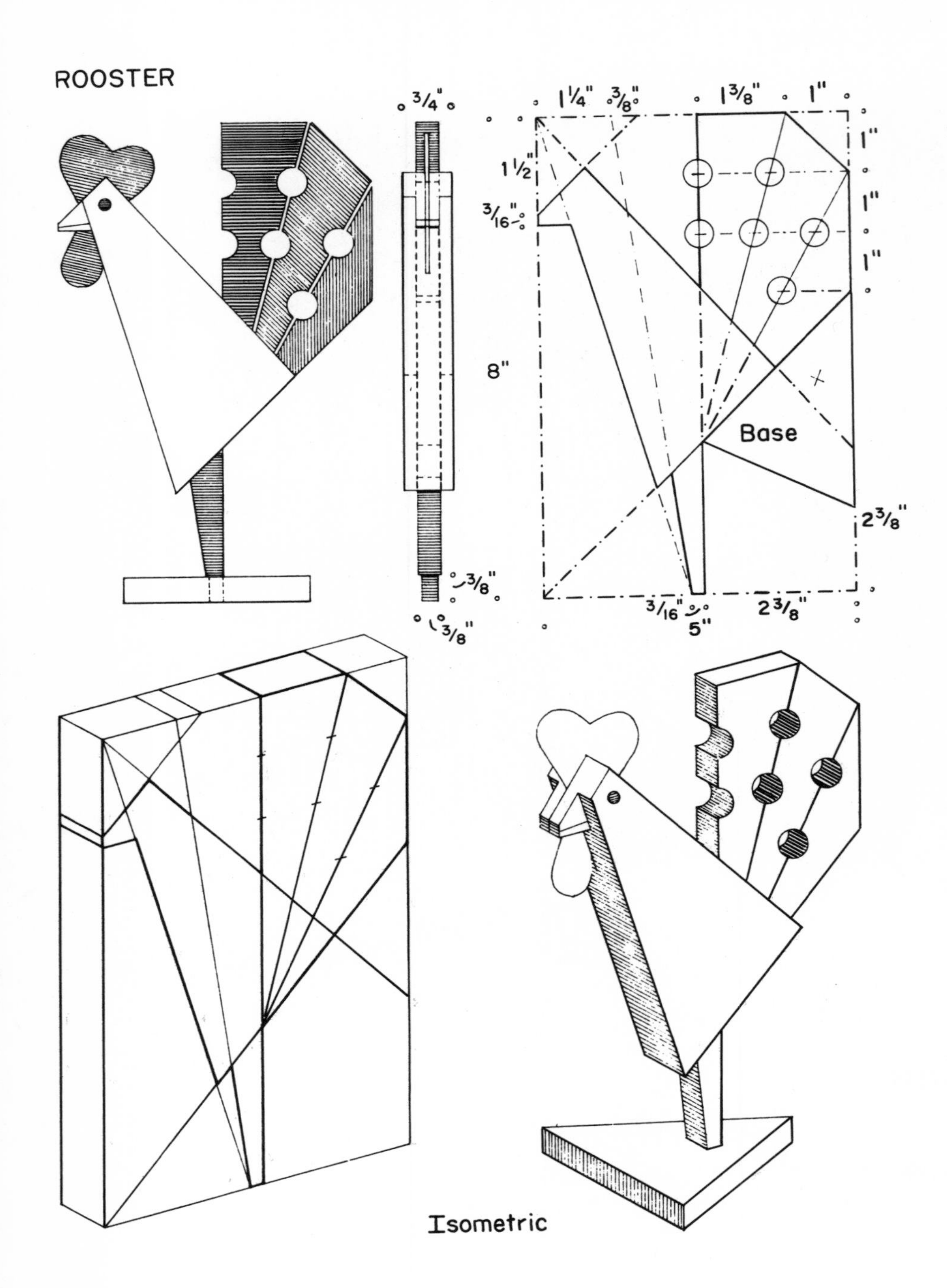

Isometric

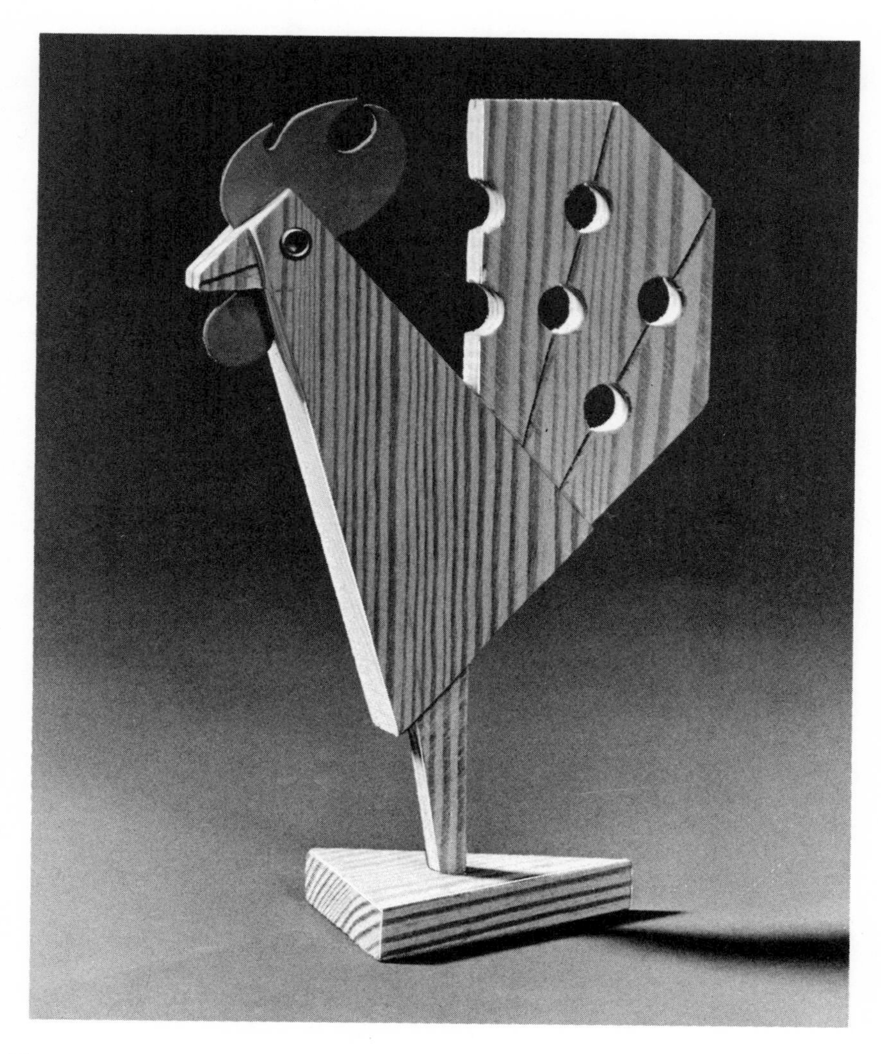

Rooster

The rooster is made in one piece and placed on a stand.

Materials Wood: ¾″ x 5″ x 8¾″ (stock 1″ x 6″) —trim to 5″.
Leather scrap for comb; eyelets for eyes.

Procedure

Cut the wood to a height of 8″. Measure off the narrow edge, square, and transfer outline onto broad surface using a ruler. Bore holes with ⅜″ auger. Saw out rooster outline and the lines in the tail down to the lowest hole.

To thin tail and leg sections, cut along each side so the middle piece is ⅜″ wide. Saw off the side pieces, first along the length, then across.

Saw a cut into the head for inserting comb.

The rooster stand is cut from waste wood as shown in drawing. Bore a 5/16″ hole in piece at X. Saw piece to half-thickness using excess waste wood for support while sawing. Then saw off excess waste wood along solid line.

The rooster's leg should fit the hole so that the back of the leg is perpendicular to the base. Glue into place. Cut the comb from a piece of cardboard or leather and glue into slot in head. Set in eyes.

The rooster is now ready for painting and decorating with plastic paint.

Elephant

The elephant is put together in several pieces, held with glue and brads.

Materials Wood: 1 5/16″ x 6″ x 5⅛″ (stock 1½″ x 8″)
Brads: ¾″ 18 ga.; 1¼″ 16 ga.; and 2″ 6d finishing nails.
Eyelets for eyes.

Procedure

Cut wood to a height of 4⅜″ and a width of 5½″. Measure off the narrow edge, square, and transfer outline onto broad surface using a ruler.

ELEPHANT

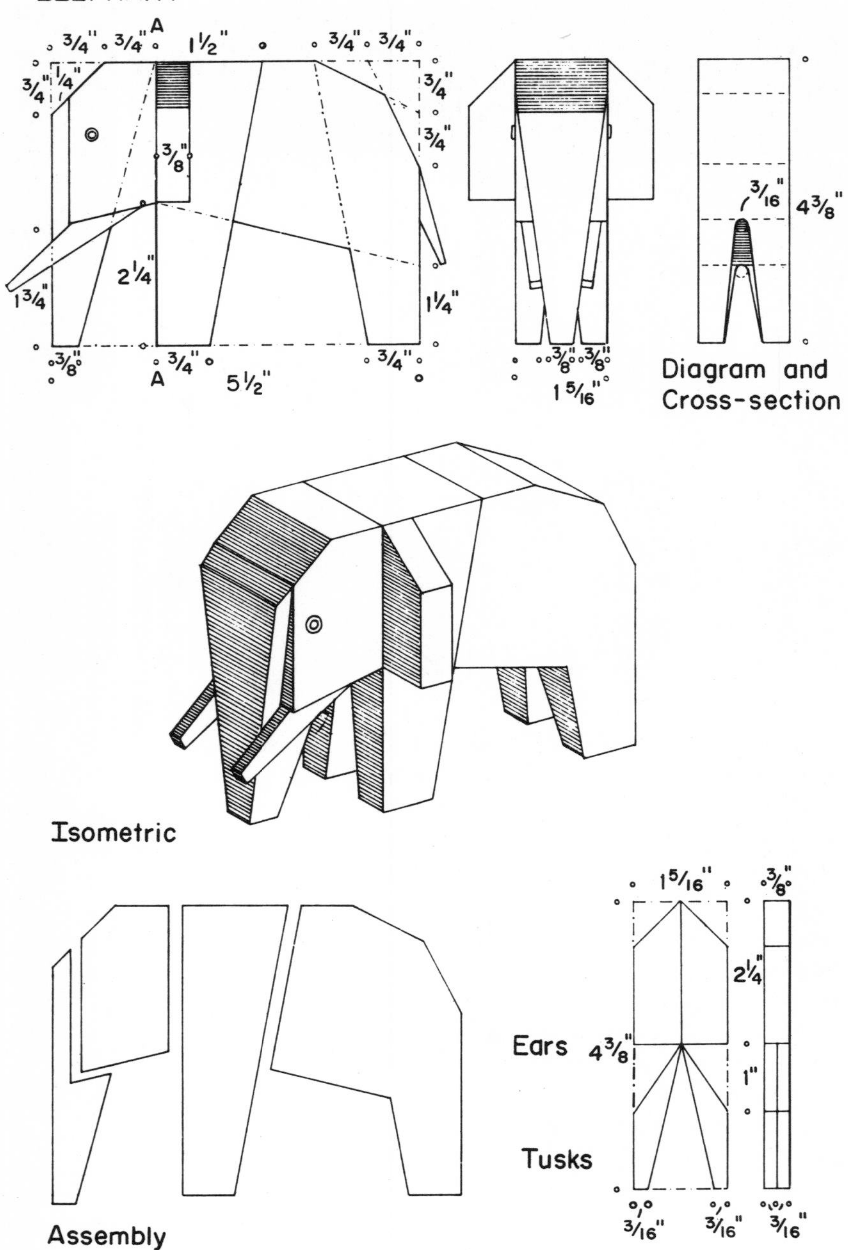
A
3/4" 3/4" 1½" 3/4" 3/4"
3/4" 1/4"
3/8"
2¼"
1¾"
1¼"
3/8"
A
3/4" 5½" 3/4"
3/8" 3/8"
1 5/16"
3/16" 4⅜"
Diagram and Cross-section
Isometric
Assembly
1 5/16" 3/8"
2¼"
Ears 4⅜"
1"
Tusks
3/16" 3/16" 3/16"

Saw the figure. Begin with the head, back, and rear legs. In order to saw the undersides of head and body, cut all the way through the figure at both sides of front legs. The trunk cannot be trimmed to proper thickness until it has been sawed away from the head. (See diagram.)

Bore a 3/16″ hole at the top of front and back legs and saw up to it to separate the legs.

Assemble the figure with glue and brads and place it in a C-clamp.

Use the extra pieces of trimmed wood to make ears and tusks as shown in drawing. As the thickness of the tusks is 3/16″, the end of the wood used in forming them should be sawed to that thickness before cutting the tusks. Of the four tusks made in this way, select the two best and use one of the others to make the tail.

Put on ears, tusks, and tail with glue and brads; apply finishing nails or eyelets for the eyes.

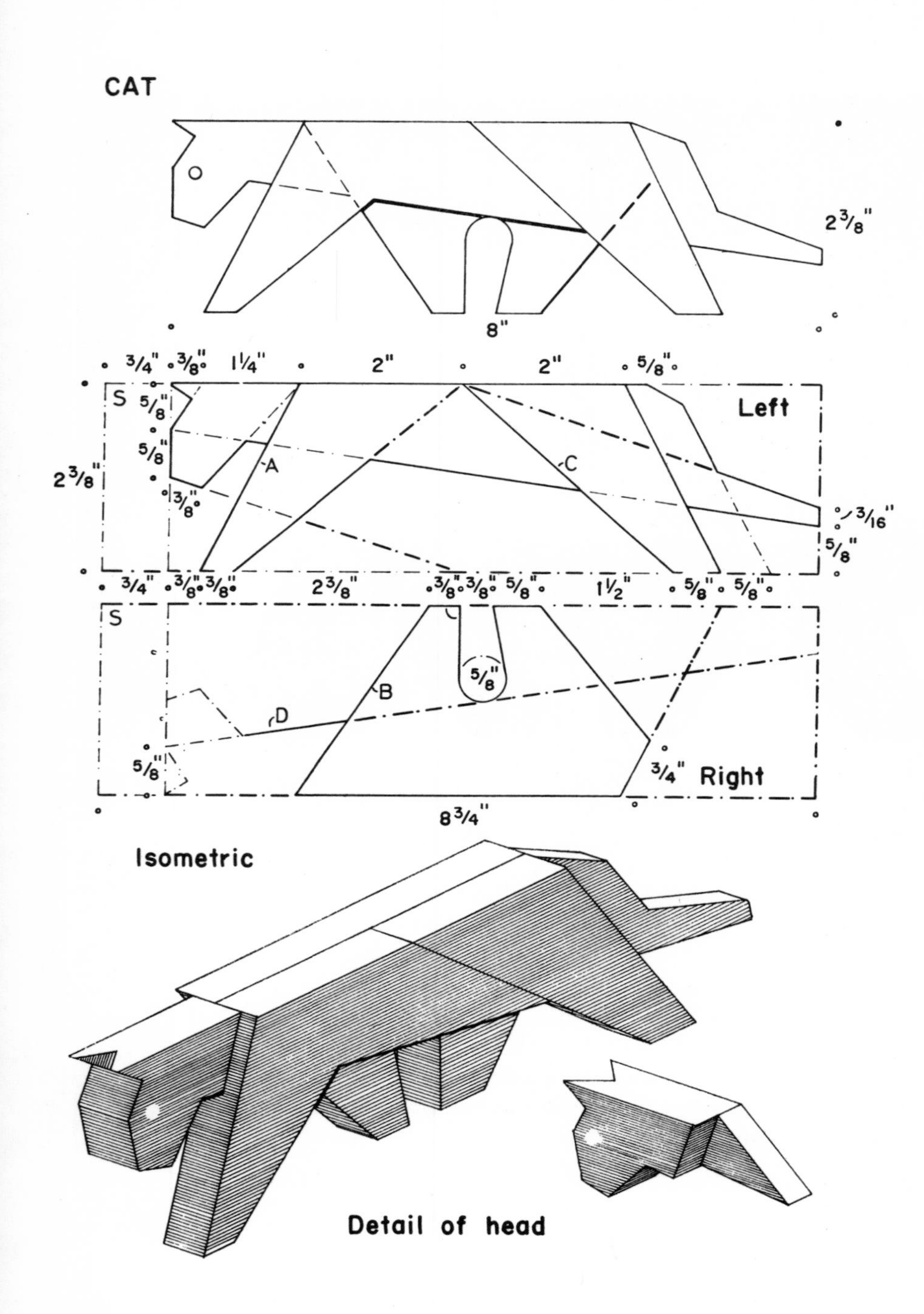
CAT
2 3/8"
8"
3/4"
3/8"
1 1/4"
2"
2"
5/8"
S
5/8"
5/8"
Left
2 3/8"
A
C
3/8"
3/16"
5/8"
3/4"
3/8"
3/8"
2 3/8"
3/8"
3/8"
5/8"
1 1/2"
5/8"
5/8"
S
5/8"
B
D
5/8"
3/4"
Right
8 3/4"
Isometric
Detail of head

Cat

As the sides of the cat are not symmetrical, it requires more complicated sawing than the other animals. In order to make the necessary lengthwise division, an extra 3/4″ is allowed in length for mounting in bench vise.

Material Wood: 1 1/16″ x 2 3/8″ x 9 1/4″ (stock 1 1/4″ x 3″) — trim to 2 3/8″

Procedure

Cut the wood to a length of 8¾″. Measure off the narrow edge, square, and transfer outline onto broad surface using a ruler. The measurements given on the diagrams are adequate.

Bore a hole in the right side so the line of the front legs and stomach are tangent to it. Bore only until the point is visible on the left side.

Mount the wood, vertically, in the front bench vise with extra mounting ¾″ piece **S** in the vise, and divide the wood through the narrow edge up to line A, along its entire length. The wood may rock back and fourth when the saw reaches the last part. Work carefully. Lay the piece on the bench and cut away the left side by sawing on line A. Then cut off the head piece by sawing the right side piece at B. Finish sawing the left side. Form the tail and saw it away from the body. In order to saw the stomach, the body must be split at C.

Finish sawing the right side.

Saw off supporting piece **S** and shape the head. Work in this order: ear, forehead, nose, lower jaw. Before sawing neck line D and letting the waste piece drop, it may be used for support while sawing a cut on each side of the head leaving the center piece ⅝″ wide. Finally, saw off waste piece **D** and the head will look as it does in the drawing.

It is preferable to assemble the pieces with glue. The body pieces should be clamped together. When the glue has set, the head and tail can be attached.

The cat may be stained or painted black with a white tip on its tail. Small brass nails can be used for eyes.

Bear

The bear's body is made in two pieces; the nose and paws being made separately and glued on.

Materials Wood: 1⅝″ x 5″ x 3½″ (stock 2″ x 6″)
Brads: ½″ 19 ga. Small nails for eyes.
Leather for ears, tongue, and tail.

Procedure

Cut the wood to a width of 4¾″ and a height of 2¾″. Measure off the narrow edge, square, and transfer outline onto broad surface using a ruler. (See diagram on page 38.)

Saw the figure. To saw under the neck the nose must first be sawed off. Shape the nose and glue it into place.

Saw a groove for the tongue and bore holes to insert ears and tail.

The paws are cut from a piece of 3/16″ wood which remains from trimming the width of the original piece. Make measurements as shown on the plan, divide the wood and cut the individual paws using a mitre box to guide the slanted cuts.

Attach paws with glue and small brads. Glue tongue, ears, and tail in slot and holes and insert the eyes close to the nose.

The bear can be made of thicker wood, for example, 2⅝″, with the head retaining its 1⅝″ width. (See photograph.)

BEAR

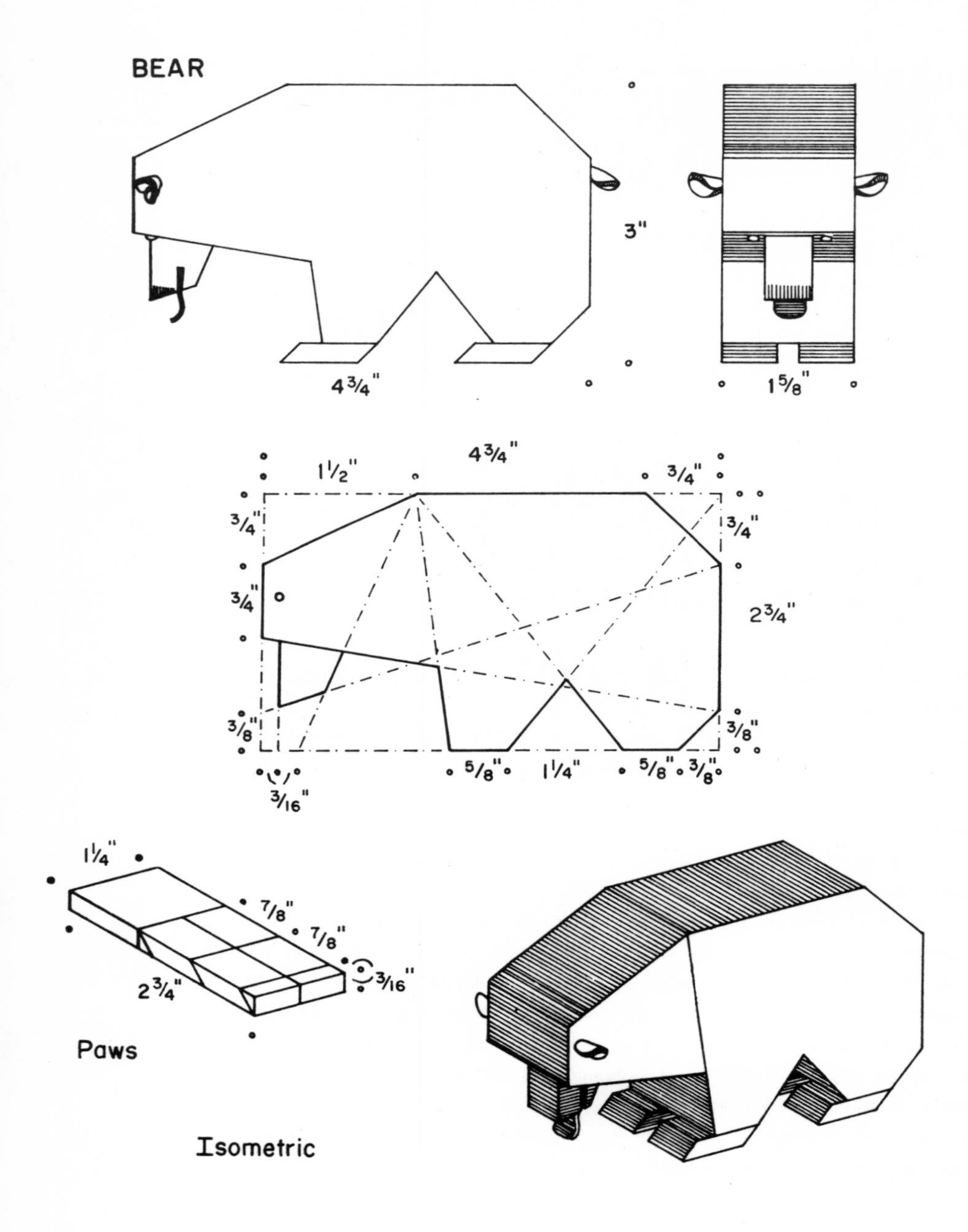

3"
4 3/4"
1 5/8"
4 3/4"
1 1/2"
3/4"
3/4"
3/4"
3/4"
2 3/4"
3/8"
3/8"
5/8"
1 1/4"
5/8"
3/8"
3/16"
1 1/4"
7/8"
7/8"
3/16"
2 3/4"
Paws
Isometric

Houses

Houses can be built in many ways and in many sizes. The examples shown here require little technical skill, but they offer the handy builder many possibilities for improvisation and variation. The subject is especially suitable for group projects where the assignment may be to construct an old town, a city, a country village, a farm, harbor, or power plant. Each participant will have a specific project to make; church, dairy or other buildings, and the surrounding area.

To make storage easier — and in cases where the joint project must be disassembled, it is best for each participant to be able to keep his own project separately boxed.

To make these shapes, a mitre box as shown in the drawing is necessary.

To assemble the various parts — house corners, units for rows of housing, the setting on of roofs, chimneys, or dormers, use brads or preferably glue. Surfaces can be smoothed with coarse sandpaper if necessary.

Materials needed besides the previously listed wood sizes include: wicker or cane for making fences, wood chips for roofs, small stones, papier mâché, and pipe cleaners for landscaping and tree trunks.

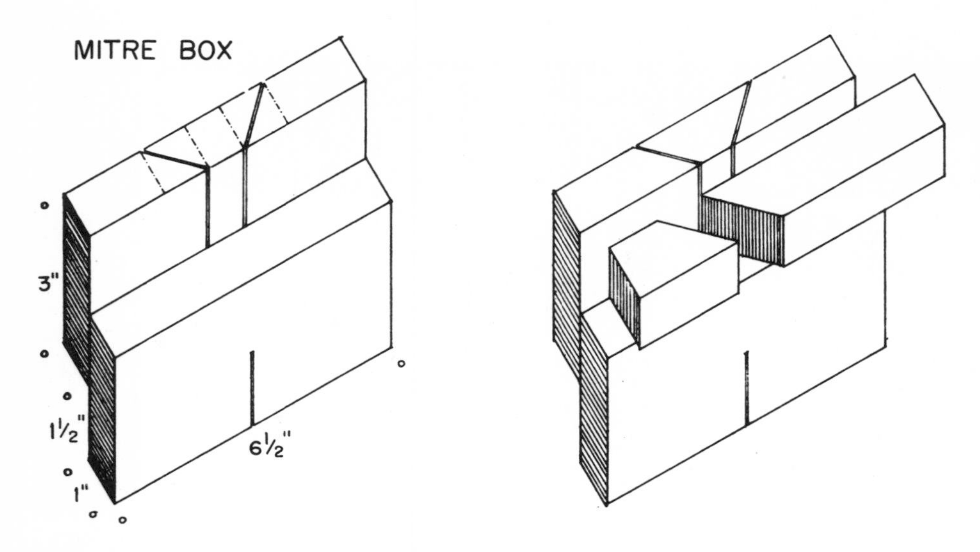

Material: 1" x 3⅛" x 13" (stock 1¼" x 3½")

Position for joining corner

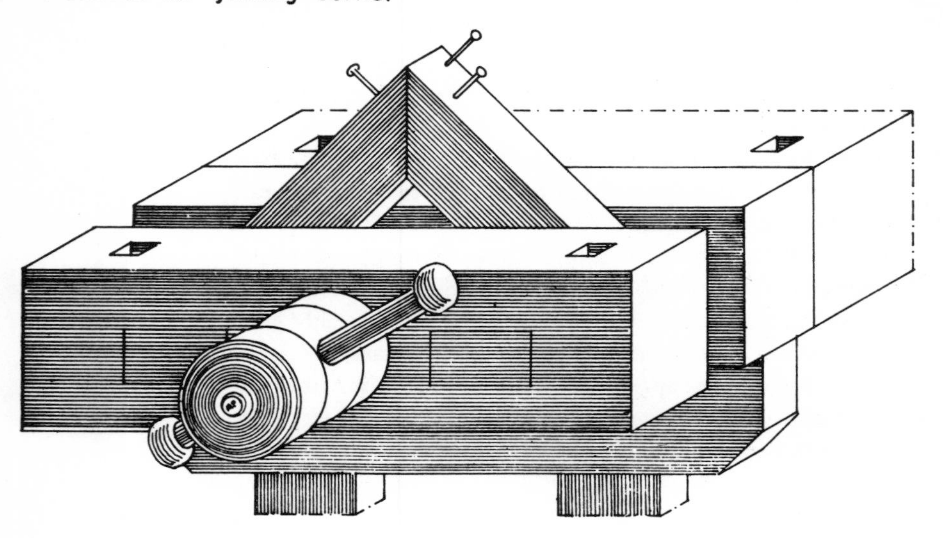

Besides ordinary papier mâché (newspaper and paste), cotton batting and glue can be used to make a faster, easier, and cleaner variety. It is more expensive but makes a good modeling material. Cut cotton in suitable size pieces (for a tree, hill, or wall), dip it in glue, work it a little with the fingers and it is ready to use. The large land formations must be built up with crumpled newspapers, wrapping paper, wood blocks, or wire cloth.

As a base for the landscape, a soft building material such as Celotex works very well. Trees and fences can be glued into holes in the surface. In order to strengthen the building base, a layer of heavy paper or cardboard can be glued underneath.

For the many model railroad builders several suitable examples and instructions for making stations, platforms, and railroad buildings are given.

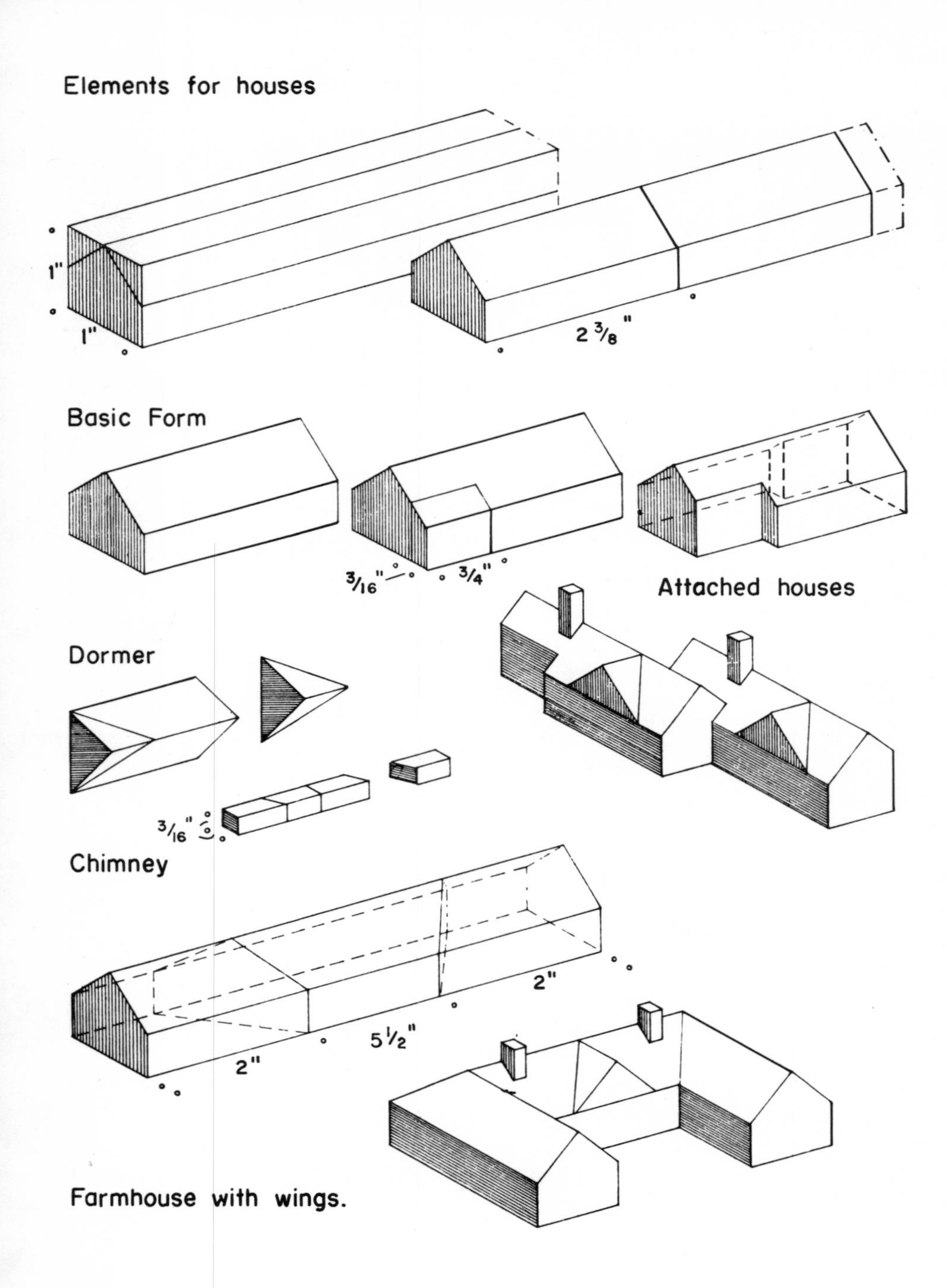
Elements for houses
1"
1"
2 3/8"
Basic Form
3/16"
3/4"
Attached houses
Dormer
3/16"
Chimney
2"
5 1/2"
2"
Farmhouse with wings.

Basic Shape and Building Elements

The building elements are made from a piece of wood that measures 1″ x 1″ in cross-section (1¼″ x 1¼″ stock). Draw a line down the middle of each of three sides, fasten the wood upright on the bench and saw one side of the roof. The other half of the roof must be sawed using the mitre box.

The piece that now remains can either be cut on an angle using the mitre box or sawed at right angles to make single houses of a given length. It can also be cut in several other ways to form a row of single or attached houses or it can be cut on a diagonal and assembled at right angles to make buildings with two or three wings.

Make the dormers out of the triangular wood piece cut from the roof. Lay it with its underside against the back surface of the mitre box and saw on the diagonal. Make the chimneys from a piece of 3/16″ x 3/16″ wood cut alternately at right angles, and on the diagonal, in the mitre box. Fasten them to the roofs with glue and an anchoring nail.

Making the elements for the houses.

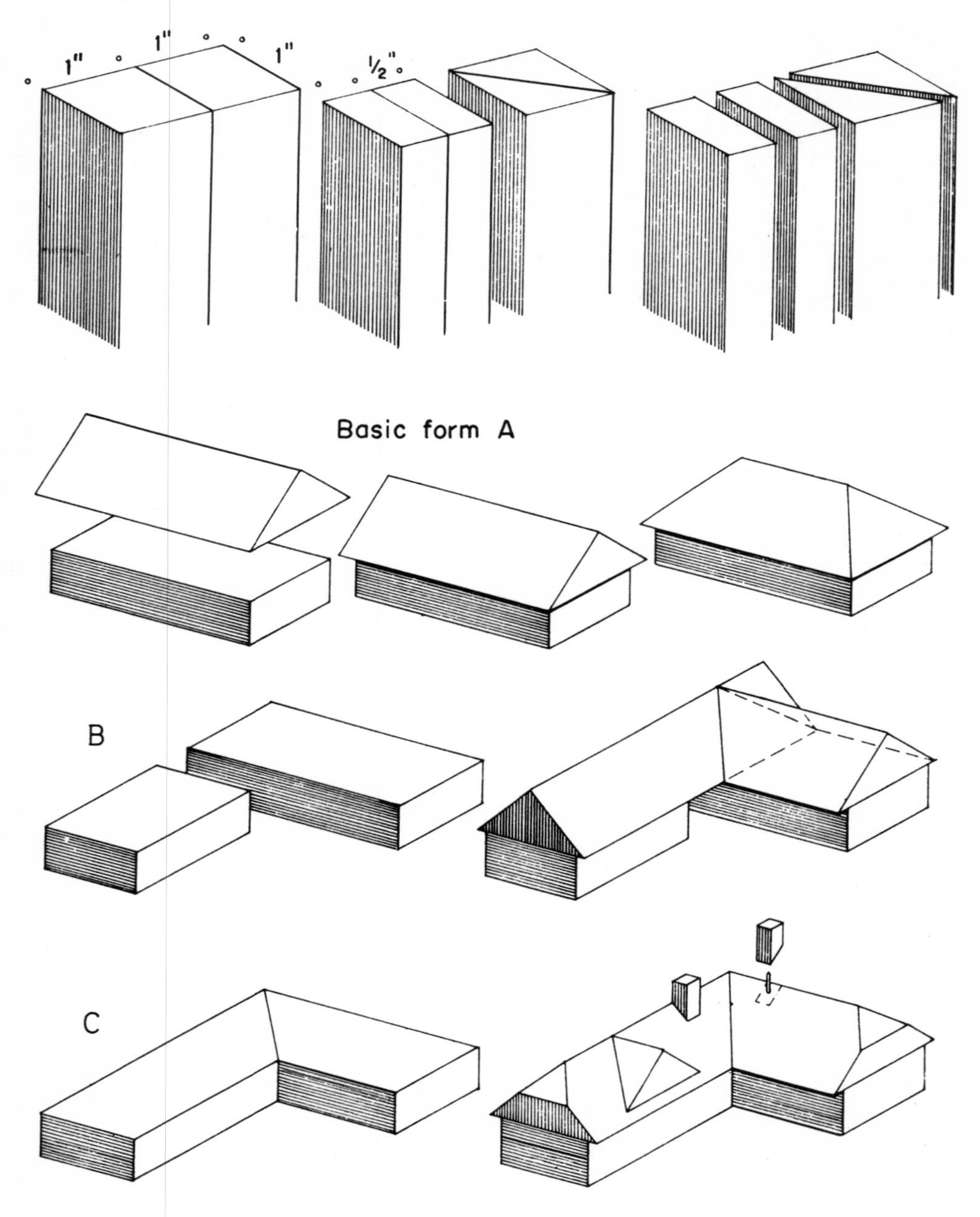

Farm Buildings

Here two shapes are needed . . . a roof element and a building element. These are made from 1″ x 2″ wood in cross-section ($1\frac{1}{4}$″ x $2\frac{1}{2}$″ stock). Saw off a segment one inch square, fasten it to the bench, then cut it across the diagonal to make two roof elements with a right angle at the roof peak. The remaining piece is the building element and can be used either as is or cut in half, lengthwise.

The building elements can be divided with either straight or diagonal cuts and assembled in various ways as in examples B and C.

Cut the roof elements in house-size segments (estimate generously because they can always be trimmed down). If the roofs are to meet in a

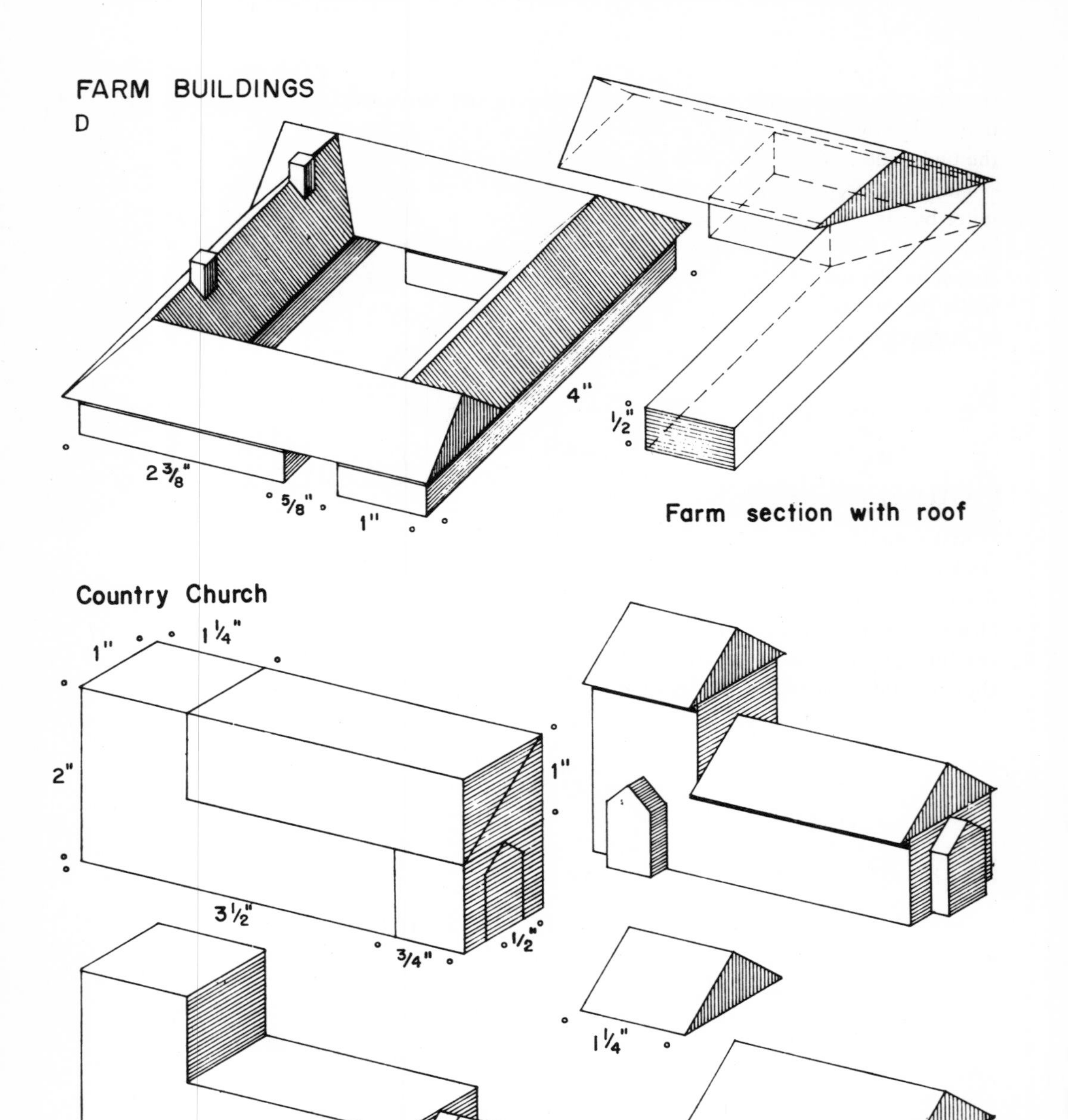
FARM BUILDINGS
D
4"
1/2"
2 3/8"
5/8"
1"
Farm section with roof
Country Church
1"
1 1/4"
2"
1"
3 1/2"
3/4"
1/2"
1 1/4"
2 3/8"

corner as in drawing C, saw them diagonally in the mitre box with the underside down. If one roof section adjoins another as in B, saw it with the underside against the back of the mitre box as if it were a long dormer.

Nail or glue the roofs, dormers, and chimneys as shown earlier. If the mitre box is not precise enough in its angles to produce pieces for a farmhouse with four wings that fit tightly at the corners, the building method shown in drawing D can be used. Here only two corners need to join, while the others are separated by doors, and the roofs support each other as in example B.

Country Church

Make the church from a piece of 1" x 2" x 4⅜" wood (1¼" x 2½" stock). Before sawing away roof elements from the building, make the diagonal saw cut with the tower section fastened to the bench for support. Shape the porch piece before sawing the back part of the church. It can be cut through twice to make matching entrance doors for the sides of the church building at the far end.

LOG CABINS

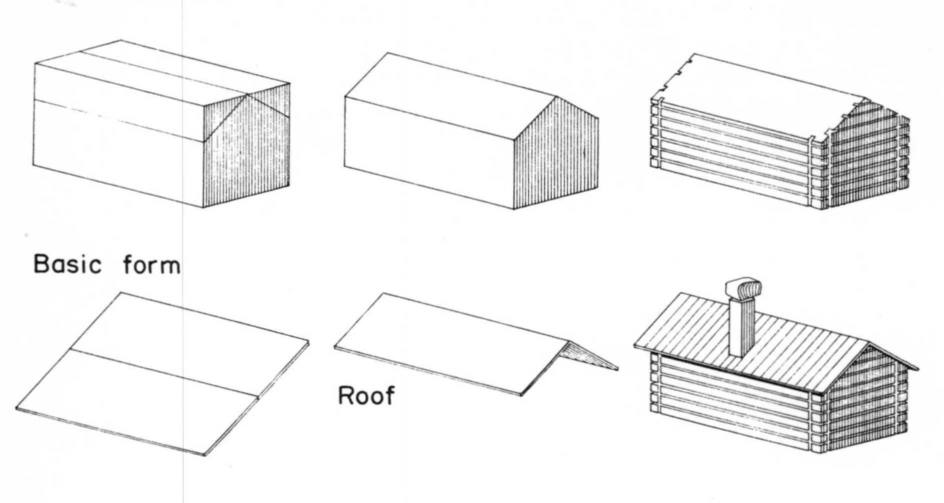

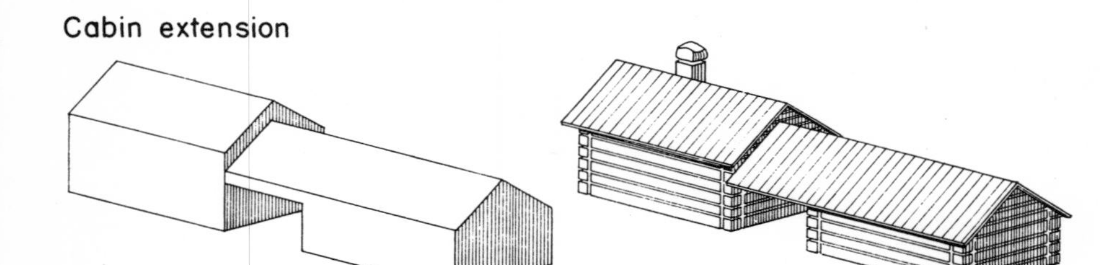

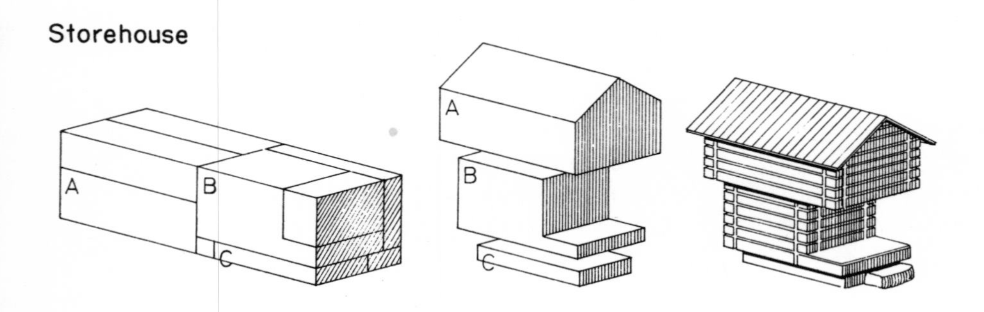

Log Cabins

The log cabins can be made from wood measuring 1″ x 1¼″ with sawed roof pieces supported by a small piece of triangular wood under the roof peak. Use the mitre box to saw parallel lines on the sides of the buildings to make them resemble log cabin construction.

Make the roof of veneer or cardboard glued together at the peak.

Matches can be used as fence posts, cane for the fencing. To further equip a farm, a well with a seesaw handle, trees, and rocks of papier mâché may be added.

OLD CITY

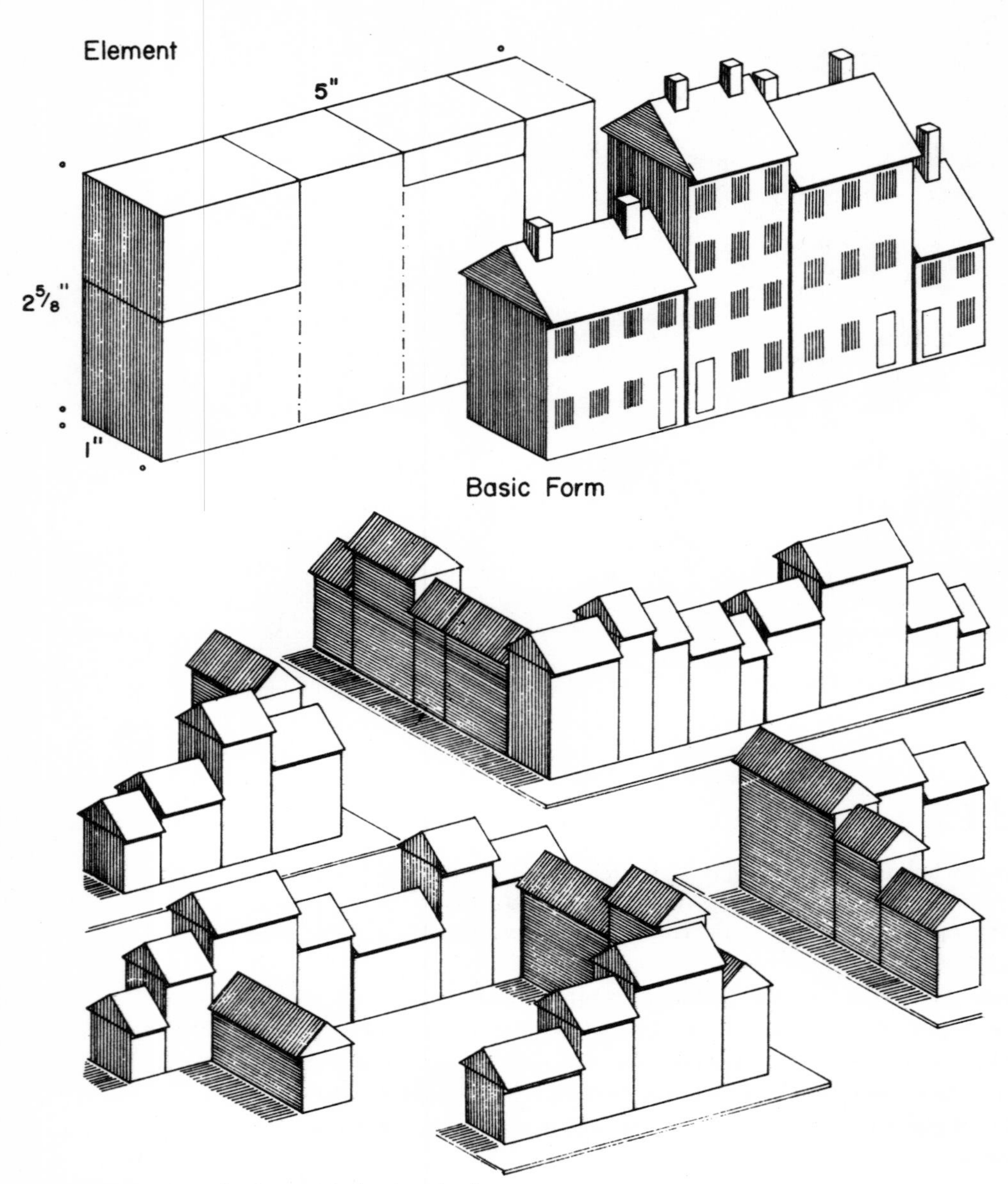

Several variations of the basic forms.

Old City

For city buildings one element made from wood measuring 1″ x 2⅝″ x 5″ (1¼″ x 3″ stock) can be used for one housing block, and a piece of 1″ x 1″ (1¼ x 1¼″ stock) wood sawed diagonally lengthwise will make the roofs.

Draw the outlines of the buildings on the broad surface and on the narrow edges. Saw out the shapes. Divisions between individual houses in a block are marked with heavy saw cuts. Cut roof pieces to fit and tack or glue in place, then add chimneys and dormers. At the street corners the building heights may vary and the roofs need not meet, in other cases the corners will need more careful attention.

Buildings for HO-gauge Model Railroads

All kinds of building types can be used for a model railroad, but a little care must be taken to make them the correct size. As a standard measurement use 1″ plus the roof height such as in the Small Town station. Larger buildings of 2, 3 or 4 stories may be 3″, 4″ or 5″ high including the roofs. The width of these houses should be about 2″, made either from one piece the width of the wood again as in the Small Town station, or by fastening two 1″ pieces together as in the Suburban station.

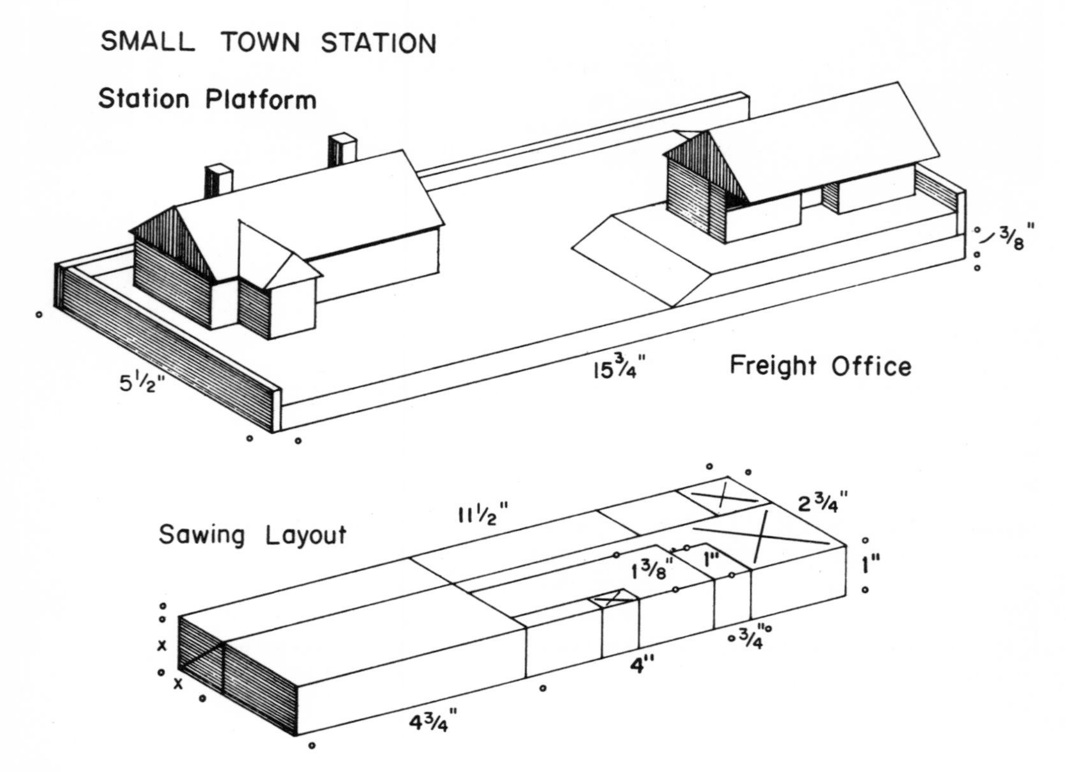

Small Town Station

This is intended to be a station in the countryside consisting of the station building and a freight office arranged on a platform. The ground under the freight office is raised to bring it up to the height of the railroad freight cars. Station signs, crates, people, and trees can be added.

Materials Base: 3/8″ x 5 1/2″ x 15 3/4″ (6″ stock)
Buildings: 1″ x 2 3/4″ x 12 1/4″ (1 1/4″ x 3 1/2″ stock)

Procedure

Buildings: Mark measurements on the narrow edge of wood, square, and continue on the broad surface where width and separation lines must be carefully drawn.

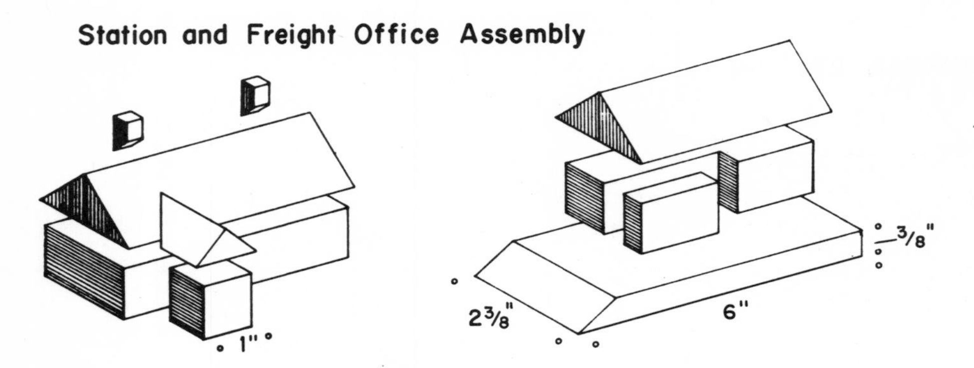

The roof elements, square in the cross-section, are first sawed off, then split on the diagonal. An extra 1¼" is allowed for fastening the piece down while sawing. From this piece the wing for the station can be made. Glue roof pieces with the most evenly cut sides together.

Saw out the building parts. If there is to be a door in the freight office, it can be made as shown in the drawing. Attach the entry wing to the station, glue on roofs and fasten houses to platform. A strip of wood can be used for a fence around the platform.

Suburban Station

This station is intended to be in a new city suburb and is modern in style. It can have several platforms and a control center with a switch tower. Paint all the sections and add typical station signs.

Materials

Station

Base: ¾" x 5½" x 15" (1" x 6" stock)

Buildings: 1" x 6" x 10⅝" (1¼" x 8" stock)

Roof: either ⅜" x 2⅜" x 18⅛" (3" stock) cut to half-thickness; or plywood 3/16" x 4¾" x 17" divided in half, lengthwise.

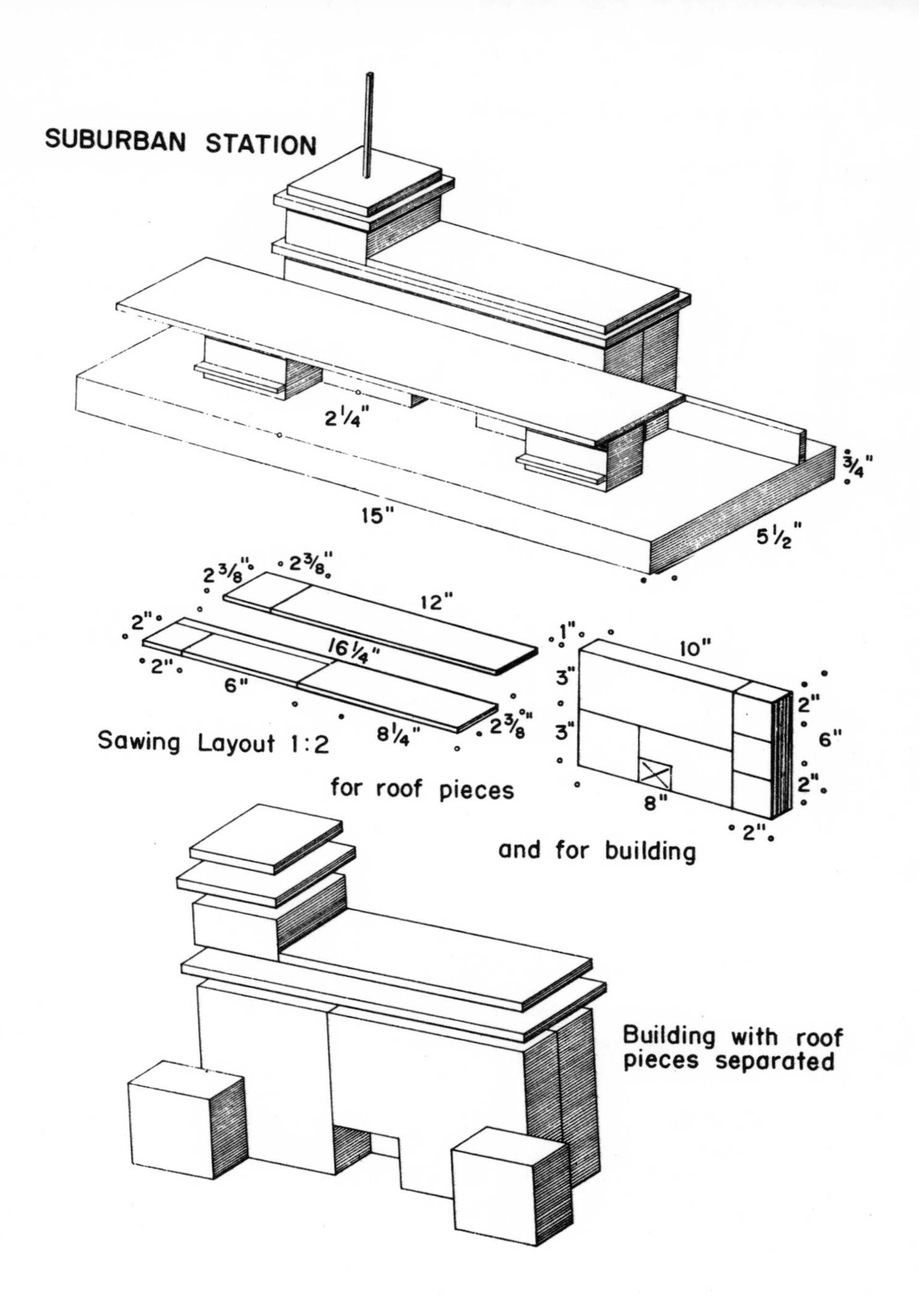
SUBURBAN STATION
2 1/4"
15"
3/4"
5 1/2"
2 3/8"
2 3/8"
12"
2"
16 1/4"
2"
6"
8 1/4"
2 3/8"
Sawing Layout 1:2
for roof pieces
1"
10"
3"
3"
2"
6"
2"
8"
2"
and for building
Building with roof pieces separated

SUBURBAN STATION

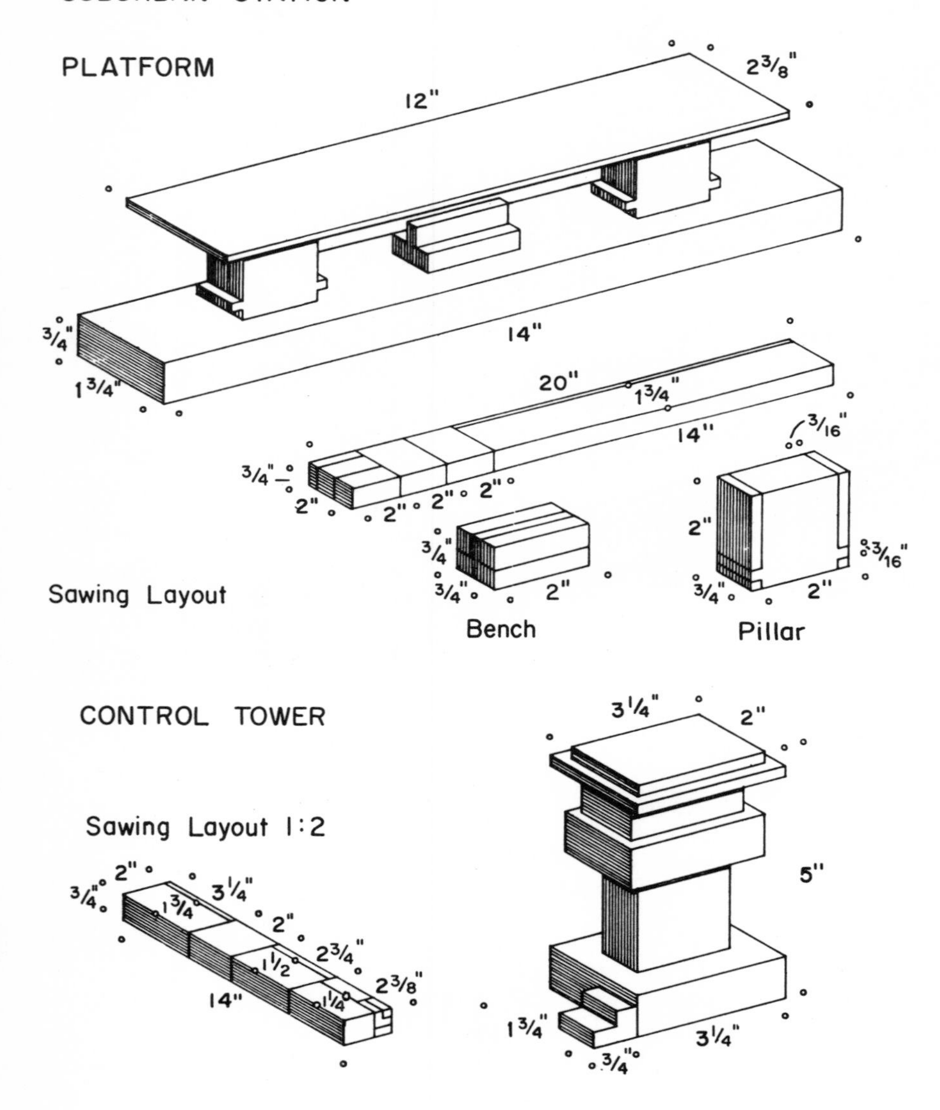

Platforms

Base piece with pillars and benches: ¾″ x 2″ x 20¾″ (1″ x 2½″ stock)
Roof: 3/16″ x 2⅜″ x 12¾″ —plywood

Control Tower

Building: ¾″ x 2″ x 15″ (1″ x 2½″ stock)
Roof: 3/16″ x 2″ x 6¾″ —plywood

Procedure

Buildings: Mark measurements on narrow edge of the wood, square, and carry measurements over to the broad surface. Then saw out the individual pieces. If the station is to have a door, cut away one piece as shown in the drawing.

The two building blocks are nailed or glued together (open sides against each other) and the newsstands which hold up the roof near the tracks are fastened to the front side. Place the building on the base. Arrange the roof sections and tower block on the building as shown in the plan. Benches, flagpole, and other details will liven up the station.

Platforms: Following the plan, cut the wood into a base piece, two columns to hold up the roof, and one lower piece for benches. The columns may be made with benches attached, but it is simpler to saw the little benches in a mitre box. Make this roof in the same way as that for the station. Assemble the parts.

Control Tower: After cutting out the individual pieces, assemble them as shown in the diagram, with nails or glue, and attach the roof.

If one has a large model railroad system, the station can be enlarged. The station shown here is considered standard minimum length. Certain standard measurements should be maintained. The base piece for the platform should not be higher than 3/4", and if one uses metal tracks the width should not exceed 1 3/4". The roof of the platform must be at least 2 3/4" above the ground and proportionately wide to the platform.

Cars and Trucks

Cars and Trucks are made from ordinary blocks of 1″ x 2″ wood stock and require only elementary sawing; lengthwise, crosswise, and diagonally through the pieces. They consist of an undercarriage, which is the same plan for all styles, and an upper part, which can be varied according to the models desired. Windows and drivers, drawn on paper can be pasted on.

Measurements for the undercarriage are given on the projection drawings. Dimensions are shown on the small isometric drawings only where there are modifications. Materials for the delivery wagon storage box, the strip on the top of the tank truck, and the firetruck ladder are not included in the plans.

HOW TO MAKE A WHEEL

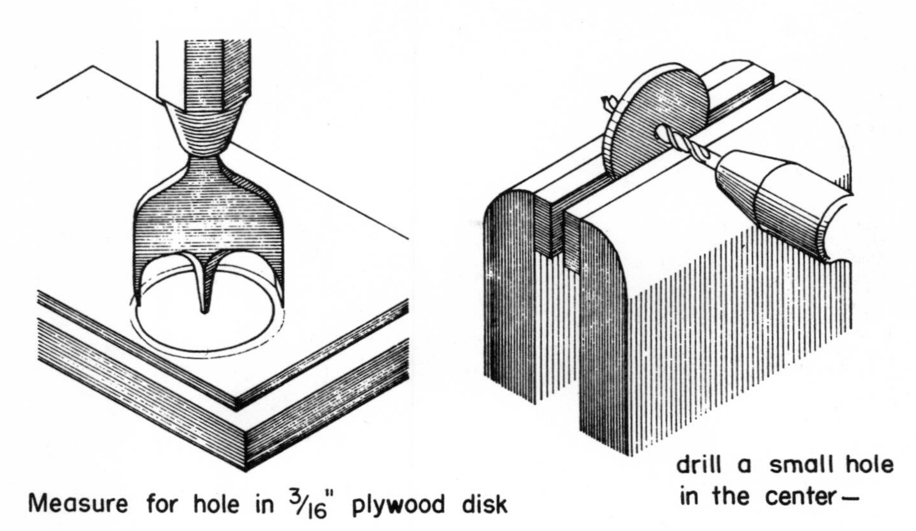

Measure for hole in 3/16" plywood disk

drill a small hole
in the center—

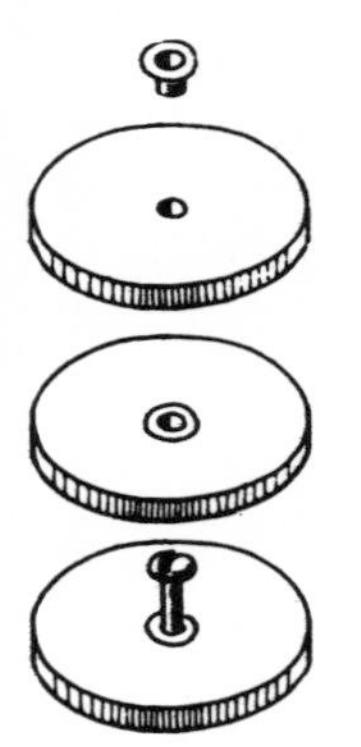

insert a 1/4" eyelet through
the front side.

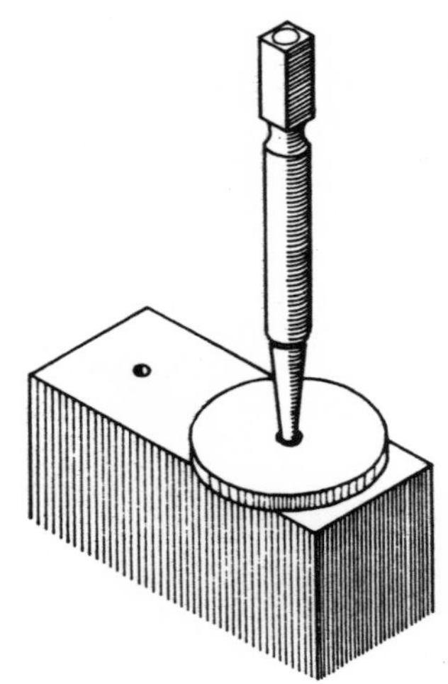

Lay wheel on an end block of wood,
and stretch eyelet out in hole with a nail set.

A roundhead screw #5 or #6 should fit.

Materials Wood: 1″ x 2″ x the length (1¼″ x 2½″ stock)
for wheels 1¼″ in diameter.
3/16″ plywood for 1¼″ wheels.
Screws: ¾″ No. 6 roundhead; 1½″ No. 6 flathead
Brads: ¾″ 18 ga., ⅞″ 17 ga.
Eyelets for wheels and lights.
Paper clips for radiator grill.

Procedure

Cut wood and draw measurements on both broad surfaces, square, and draw outline on narrow edge, using a ruler. (See drawings, pages 62–63.)

Saw all the individual parts away from each other and shape them. Begin with lengthwise saw cuts wherever possible (bumper, truck body, etc.) then saw crosswise and diagonally.

When the parts are finished, assemble them with screws inserted through the undercarriage or with brads. Bore through the wheels and mount them using a nail set. (See page 60.) Attach them to the cab or truck body, together with lights and grill.

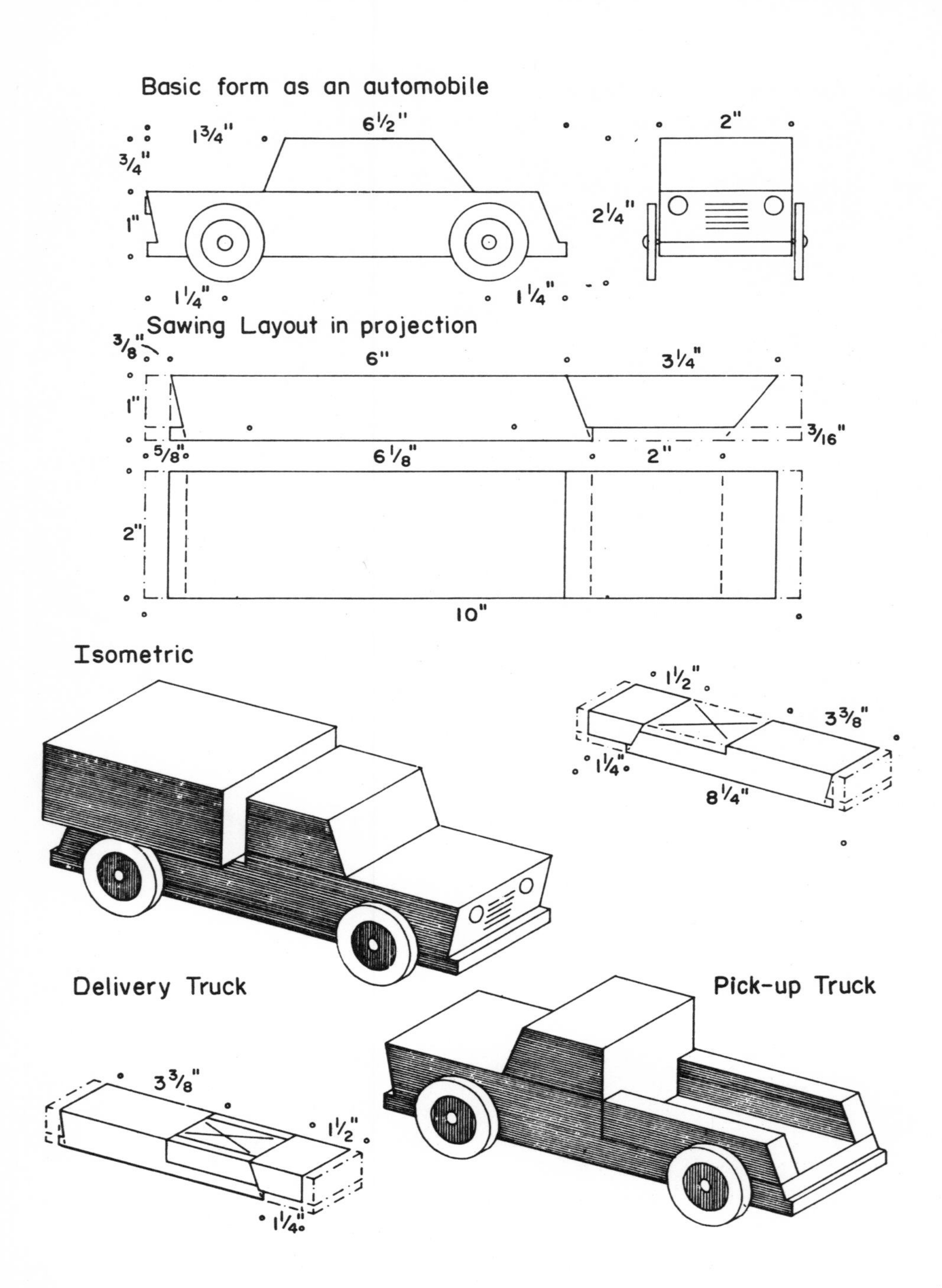
Basic form as an automobile
1¾"
6½"
¾"
1"
1¼"
1¼"
2"
2¼"
Sawing Layout in projection
⅜"
6"
3¼"
1"
3/16"
5/8"
6⅛"
2"
2"
10"
Isometric
1½"
3⅜"
1¼"
8¼"
Delivery Truck
Pick-up Truck
3⅜"
1½"
1¼"

Basic form as a Tank Truck

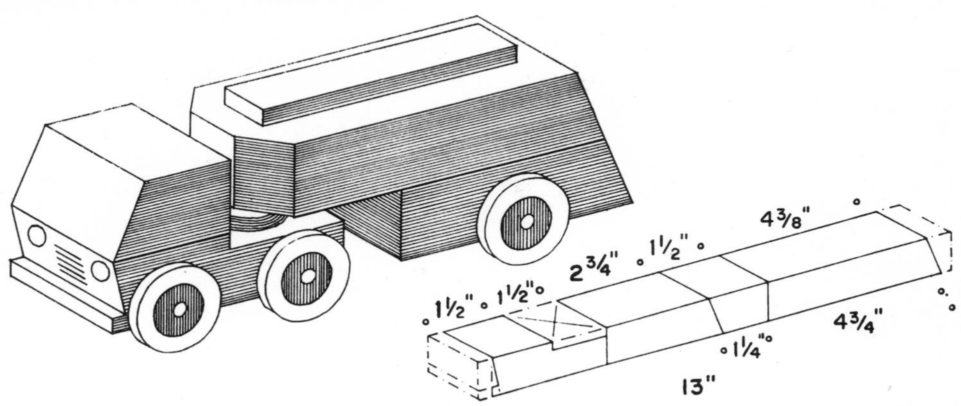

– as a Fire Truck

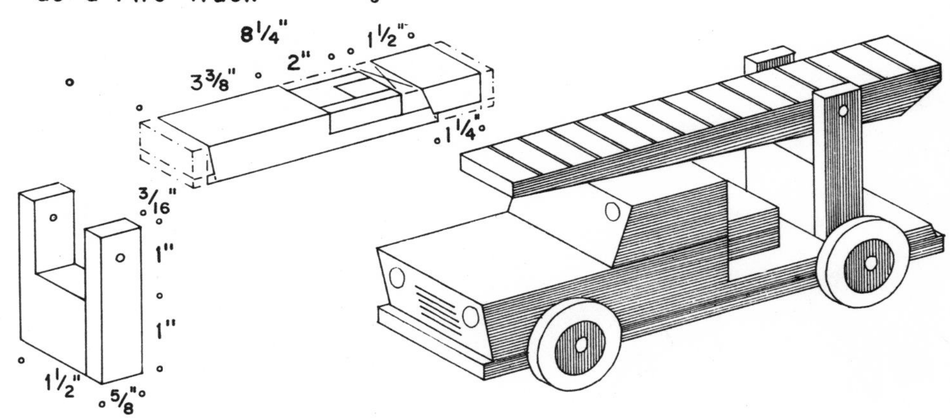

– as an Ambulance

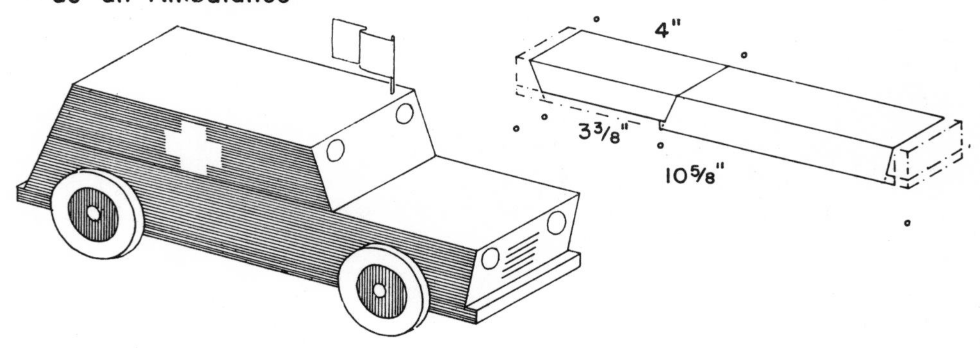

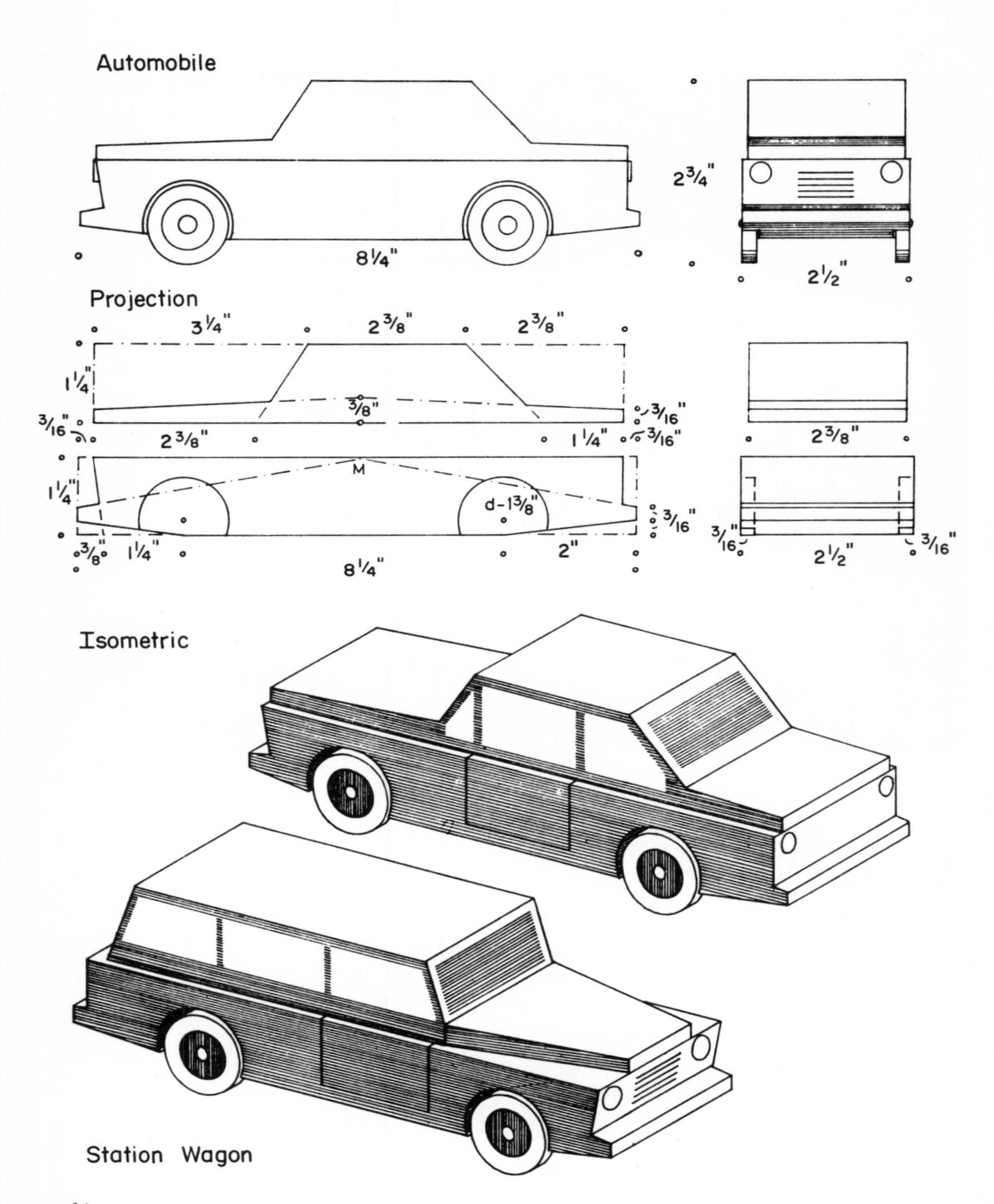
Automobile
8 1/4"
2 3/4"
2 1/2"
Projection
3 1/4"
2 3/8"
2 3/8"
1 1/4"
3/8"
3/16"
2 3/8"
1 1/4"
3/16"
3/16"
2 3/8"
M
1 1/4"
d-1 3/8"
3/16"
3/8"
1 1/4"
2"
8 1/4"
3/16"
2 1/2"
3/16"
Isometric
Station Wagon

Automobiles

The automobiles are made from a board 1¼″ thick and 5″ wide which is divided lengthwise into two parts; one for the top and one for the bottom. The top piece should be 3/16″ to ¼″ smaller than the base. The wheels are recessed into the sides of the cars.

Because of the width of the wood and the many angular saw cuts, it may be helpful to use a ¾″ board as a support in sawing.

The undercarriage is the same in the two isometric drawings, while the top can be varied in many ways. Copy the advertisements for styles.

Materials Wood: 1¼″ x 5″ x 9¼″ (1½″ x 6″ stock)
3/16″ to ¼″ plywood for four 1¼″ wheels.
Screws: ¾″ No. 6 roundhead; 1½″ No. 6 flathead.
Eyelets for wheels and lights, paper clip for radiator grill.

Procedure

Divide the wood lengthwise so that one piece is about 3/16″ narrower than the other. (See the top drawing on the right, page 64.)

Cut the widest piece for the undercarriage 8¼″ in length. Draw the measurements on its top and bottom; square, and transfer the outline with positioning of wheels, using a ruler.

Bore out the holes for the wheels with a 1⅜″ auger as deep as the wheels are thick. To prevent splintering, use a piece of supporting wood against the bottom of the car piece.

After boring is completed, saw front and back, making the lengthwise saw cuts first. In making the difficult angular cuts use a piece of supporting wood.

To make the car top, use the narrower piece of wood, trim it down so that the length corresponds to the finished undercarriage. Mark the measurements, square, and draw the outline, then saw.

Bore holes in the undercarriage for the screws and assemble the pieces.

Bore through the wheels and mount them using eyelets (See page 60.) and screw them in place. Put on lights and radiator grill.

Car may be painted with plastic paint.

Delivery Truck

This model is made for the most part just as the preceding ones and can be loaded with any small cargo. In order to make the recessed front and open rear deck, a piece must be sawed from each side in order to form the forward recess. The rear of the truck can be cut with an open rear deck for the pick-up model-A, or squared, for the panel truck-B.

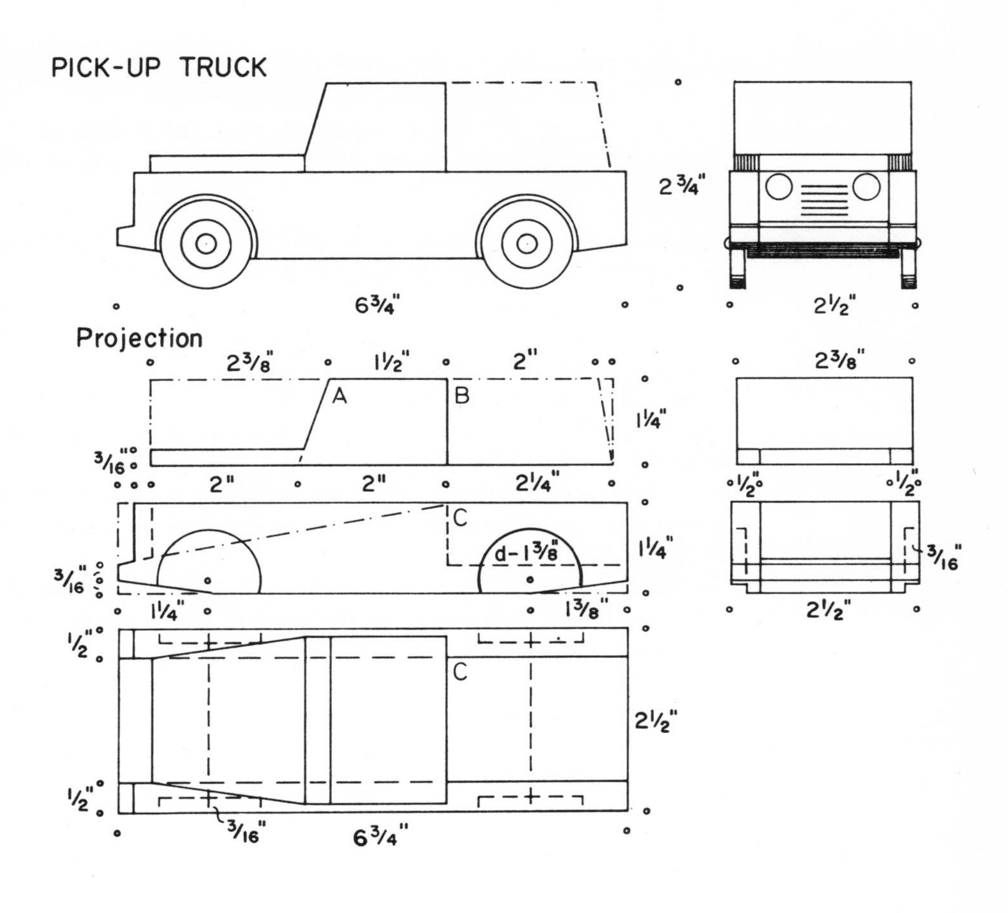
PICK-UP TRUCK
6 3/4"
2 3/4"
2 1/2"
Projection
2 3/8"
1 1/2"
2"
A
B
1 1/4"
3/16"
2"
2"
2 1/4"
C
d-1 3/8"
1 1/4"
3/16"
1 1/4"
1 3/8"
2 3/8"
1/2"
1/2"
3/16"
2 1/2"
1/2"
C
2 1/2"
1/2"
3/16"
6 3/4"

Isometric

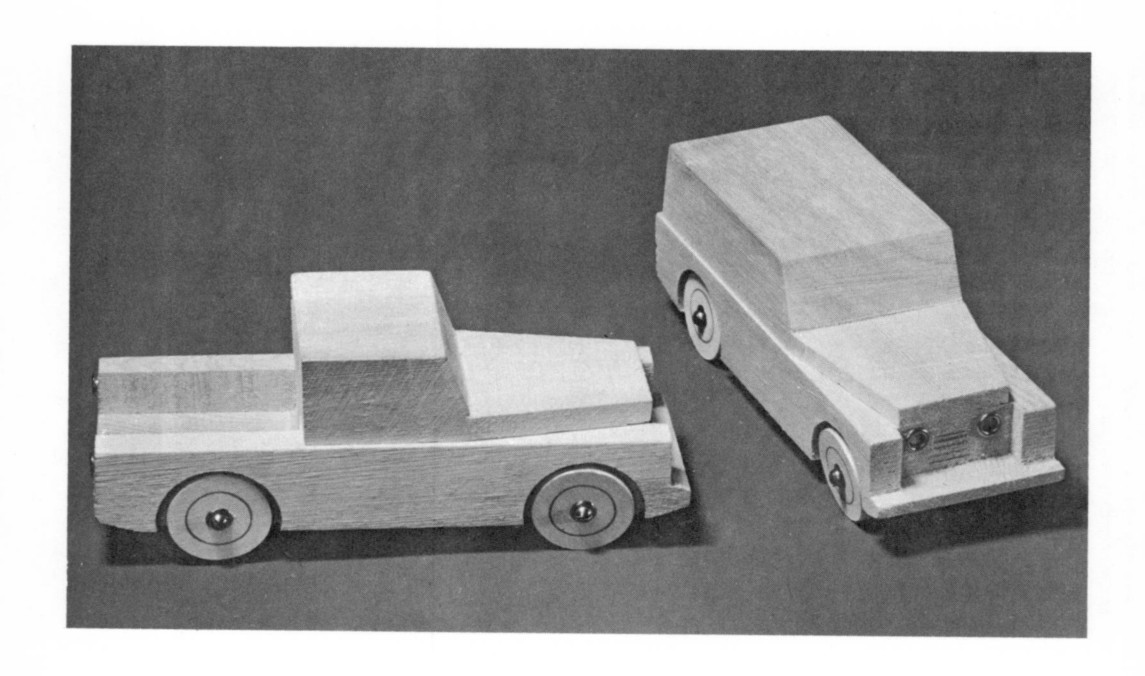

Materials

Wood: 1¼″ x 5″ x 7½″ (1½″ x 6″ stock)
3/16″ to ¼″ plywood for four 1¼″ wheels.
Screws: ¾″ No. 6 roundhead; 1½″ No. 6 flathead.
Brads: ⅞″ 17 ga.
Eyelets for wheels and lights, paper clips for radiator grill.

Procedure

Follow the procedure given on page 66. When the undercarriage has been drawn and sawed out, a ½″ piece is cut away from each side, lengthwise. Shape the center section. Saw out piece C if the truck is to have an open rear deck.

Glue the side strips back into place. Side wheels can be nailed into place.

Finish the top of the truck and screw it to the undercarriage as was done with the automobiles.

Trains

Switch Engine

The switch engine is built of three blocks of wood, nailed and screwed together. Roof and sides are nailed on after assembly.

Materials Boiler: 2″ x 2″ x 9¼″ (2½″ x 2½″ stock)
Middle, bottom pieces, and smokestack: 1″ x 3⅝ x 11″ (1¼″ x 4″ stock)
Sides, roof, etc.: ⅜″ x 3″ x 18⅞″ (3½″ stock)
3/16″ plywood for four 2″ wheels and one 1¼″ wheel.
Screws: ¾″ No. 6 roundhead; 1½″ No. 6 flathead
Brads: ¾″ 18 ga.; ⅞″ 17 ga.; 1¼″ 16 ga.; and 2″ 6d finishing nails
Thumb tacks for shock absorbers, and eyelets for wheels.

Procedure

Boiler: Draw lines for boiler and tender. Saw slanted edges of boiler, but omit the tender until the sides are attached.

Middle and bottom pieces, etc.: Divide the piece lengthwise as shown in plan, draw the outline, and cut pieces.

The little middle piece M in the engineer's cab should be cut down to a thickness of ⅝″ before sawing it away from E.

Divide middle piece E crosswise, and shape the front part of it. The center part should be the same width as bottom piece F (1½″). Mark the position of the wheels on piece F, and bore holes for assembly screws which join F to E.

Divide smokestack piece, lengthwise, to a ¾″ thickness, before sawing it away from F.

Cut out smokestack and tanks. Saw off slanted edges before sawing away waste wood.

SWITCH ENGINE

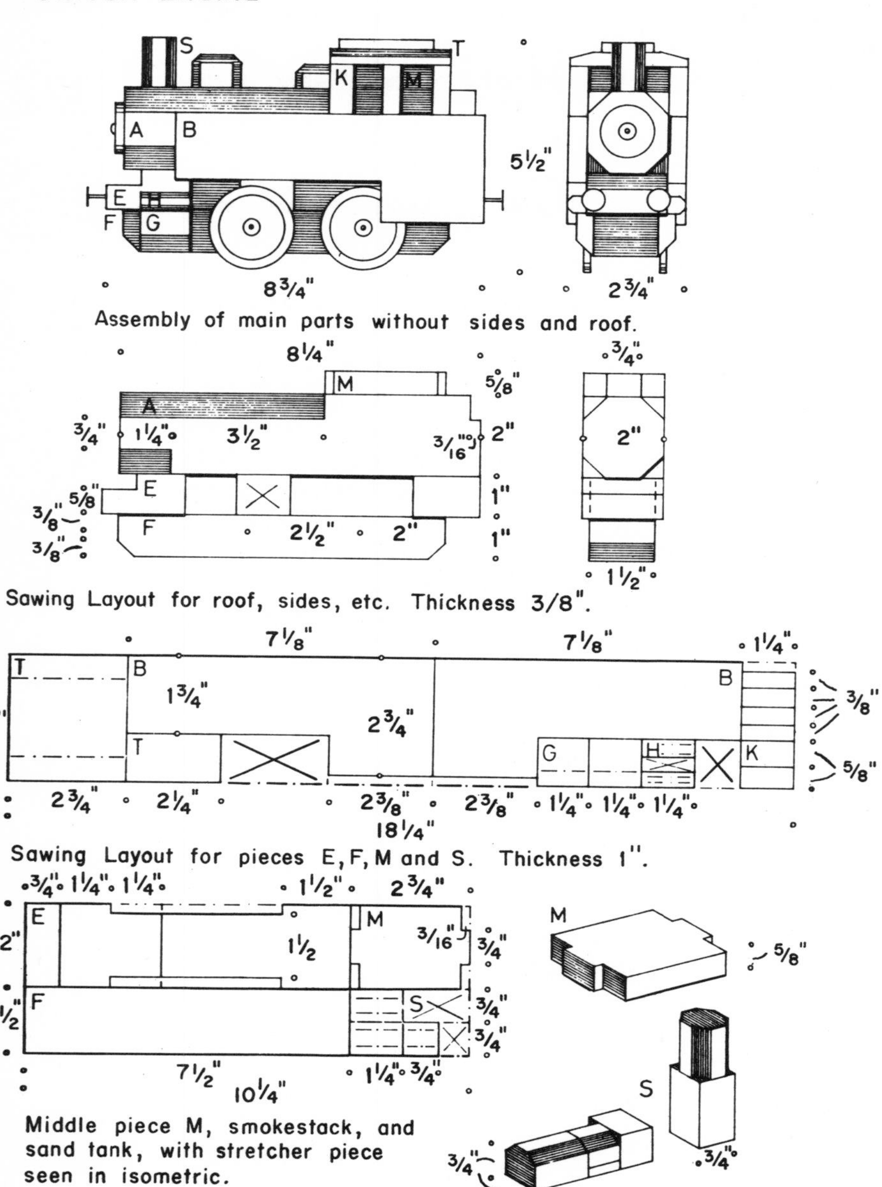

Assembly of main parts without sides and roof.

Sawing Layout for roof, sides, etc. Thickness 3/8".

Sawing Layout for pieces E, F, M and S. Thickness 1".

Middle piece M, smokestack, and sand tank, with stretcher piece seen in isometric.

Sides, roof, etc.: Draw patterns following plan and cut out the individual pieces. Saw slanted edges of the large roof section T, before sawing it away from piece B.

Trim the small roof piece T to half-thickness, lengthwise, before sawing away the waste.

It is easier to saw slanted edges of cylinder pieces G and H before they are cut apart.

Assembly: Screw the middle piece E under the boiler and then attach bottom piece F.

Nail piece M to boiler with cab and roof over it.

When the roof and side pieces B are against it, the small division at K can be made.

Then saw out the tender so it is flush with the rear side pieces.

Attach the smokestack, tanks, etc.

(The smokestack and tanks can be screwed down upon a narrow screw which has had the head removed and is placed upside down in a hole in the wood, so that the screw threads protrude. A little glue will hold it firm.)

Wheels: Bore through wheels and set them in place. If the wheels are thicker than the 3/16″ space allowed where the back part of the side piece B covers the rear wheels, the width of the bottom piece F, and its corresponding part on middle piece E, must be altered until there is enough space for them to rotate.

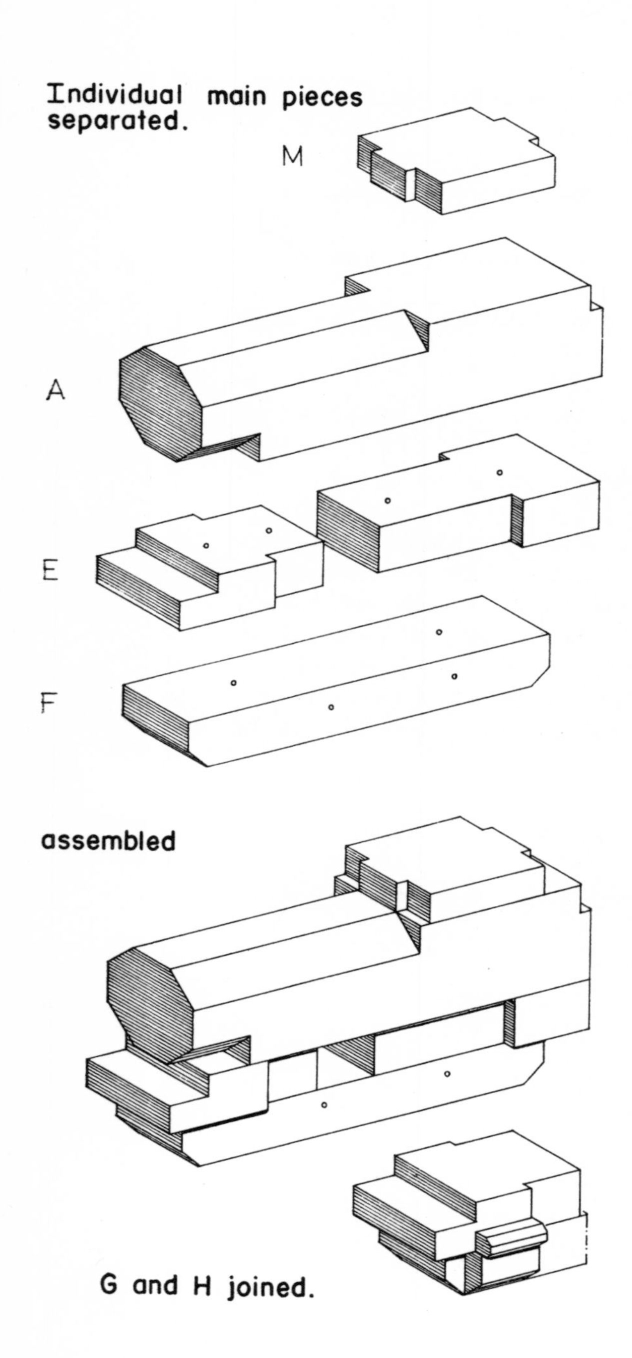
Individual main pieces separated.
M
A
E
F
assembled
G and H joined.

PASSENGER CAR

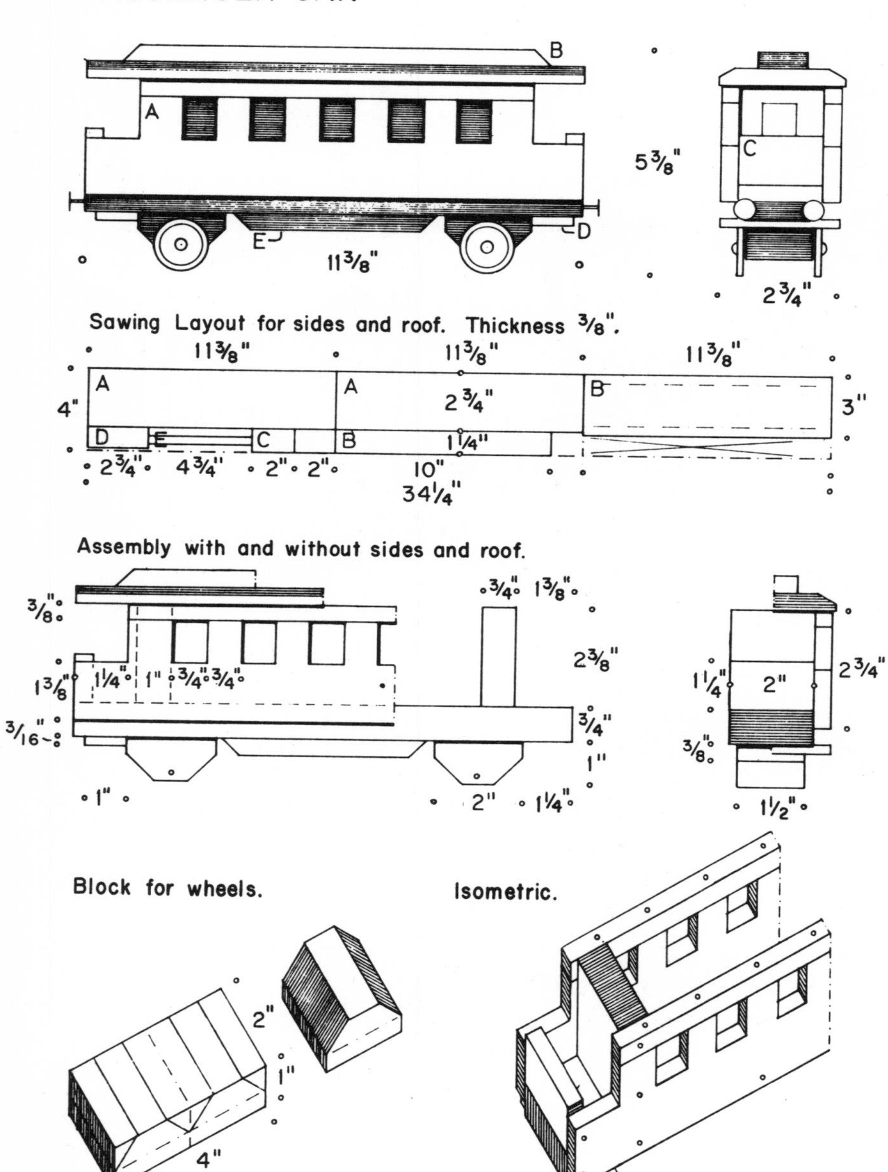

Passenger Car

The passenger car is built up over a base on which two blocks of equal size and width are arranged as end pieces in the enclosed part of the car. The sides and roof are nailed on this frame after they have been shaped, following the drawing. Make three or more cars for a nice long train.

Materials Bottom and end pieces: 3/4″ x 2″ x 17″ (1″ x 2 1/2″ stock)
Sides, roof, etc.: 3/8″ x 4″ x 35″ (5″ stock)
Blocks for wheels: 1 3/8″ x 2″ x 4 3/4″ (1 1/4″ x 2 1/2″ stock)
3/16″ plywood for four 1 1/4″ wheels
Screws: 3/4″ No. 6 roundhead; 1 1/2″ No. 6 flathead
Brads: 7/8″ 17 ga.; and 1 1/4″ 16 ga.
Thumb tacks for shock absorbers; eyelets for wheels; and upholstery nails.

Procedure

Bottom and end pieces: Divide the wood crosswise into three pieces. The piece 11⅜″ long is for the bottom, and that 4¾″ long will be the two end pieces which are nailed to the base. Cut out the wheel blocks and screw them to the bottom.

Sides and roof: Draw the outline, following the plan and cut the wood. Before the big roof piece B, is sawed away from A, saw slanted edges so that A can be used for support.

Trace side A. Saw off the piece over the windows. Then saw the vertical lines and chip away the extra wood along the perpendicular line with a small, sharp chisel.

Nail piece from above the windows back into place. Nail the sides of the coach to the frame so that the projecting end piece fits flush with each of the fixed end pieces.

Put the low end pieces C, into place.

Mitre the ends of the small roof and fasten it to the main section.

Nail the assembled roof to the sides and fixed end pieces.

Cars steps, etc.: Before sawing car steps D, from E, divide piece, lengthwise, to half-thickness, using piece E as a prop. The piece is placed tightly up against the wheel block.

Divide piece E, lengthwise, mitre ends and place on car bottom section as reinforcement.

Screw on the wheels.

Put on shock absorbers about 1½″ apart.

Painting: Passenger car can be painted with plastic paint; the base reaching up to the side pieces, with the roof and interior in black. The sides and ends should also be painted in a color.

The sides may be decorated with pen lines.

Express Locomotive

The locomotive is made of four blocks, nailed and screwed together. After this assembly the roof and sides are nailed on.

Materials Boiler and Tender: 2″ x 2″ x 17″ (2½″ x 2½″ stock)
Sides, roof, and middle piece D: ⅜″ x 6″ x 20″ (8″ stock)
or (3½″ stock — 40″ long)
Base and middle piece E. 1″ x 4″ x 16½″ (1¼″ x 5″ stock)
or (2½″ stock — 33″ long)
3/16″ plywood for six 2″ wheels, and eleven 1¼″ wheels.
Screws: ¾″ No. 6 roundhead; 1½″ No. 6 flathead
Brads: ¾″ 18 ga.; ⅞″ 17 ga.; 1¼″ 16 ga.; and 2″ 6d finishing nails
Thumb tacks for shock absorbers; eyelets for wheels.

EXPRESS LOCOMOTIVE

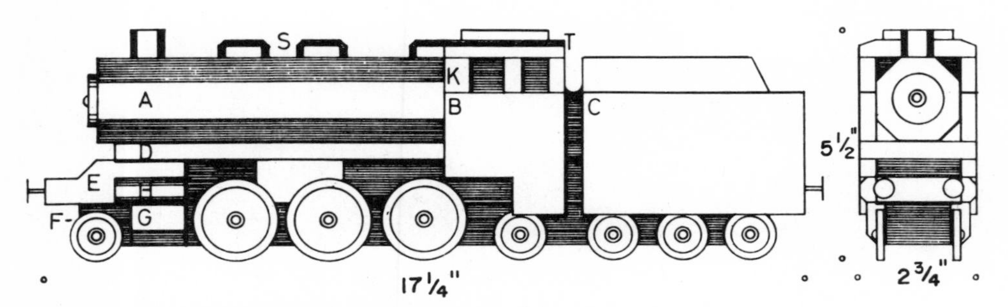

Assembly without sides and details.

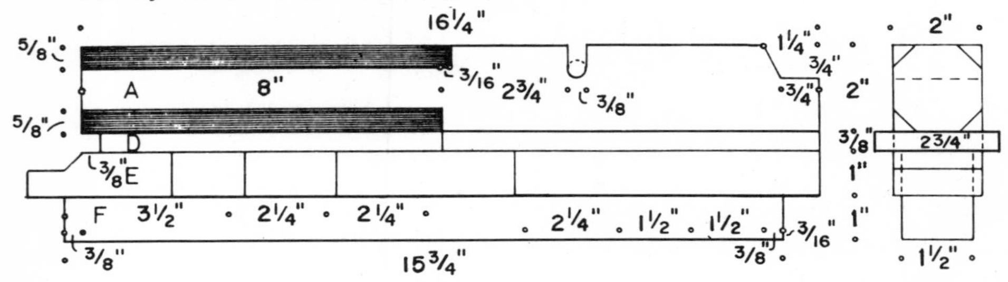

Sawing Layout for middle piece D, sides, etc. Thickness 3/8".

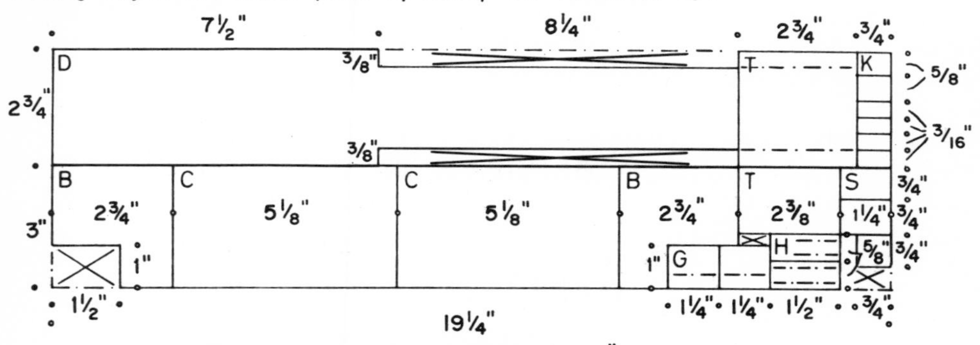

Middle piece E before dividing. Thickness 1".

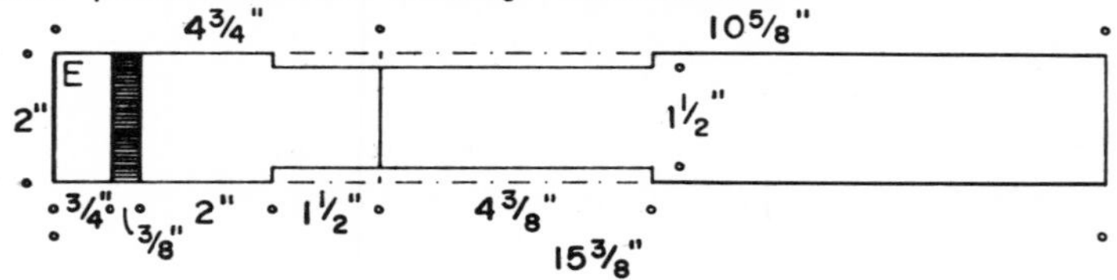

Procedure

Boiler: Draw lines for slanted edges of boiler with the top 3/16" longer than the bottom, to the hole between the engineer's cab and the coal tender, and the tender's rear section.

Cut off corners to make slanted edges, bore hole and make saw cuts behind cab; saw tender.

Side, roof, and piece D: Draw outline on wood following plan, divide piece lengthwise, and make the individual pieces as follows:

Saw the small window parts at K.

Cut slanted edges on the large roof piece T, before sawing off piece D.

Make middle piece D.

Tanks S, and cylinder pieces G and H, are made using the mitre box.

Divide the small roof section lengthwise, to half-thickness, before sawing it from B, which may then be used as a prop.

Assembly: Nail middle piece D under boiler, and nail roof piece to top.

Position K pieces upright against roof to make window divisions.

Nail on side pieces B and C.

Base and center piece E: Divide piece lengthwise, into center piece E, and base piece F.

Cut center piece crosswise and saw out shape. Attach with screws under D.

Mark positions for wheels on base piece and screw it beneath E.

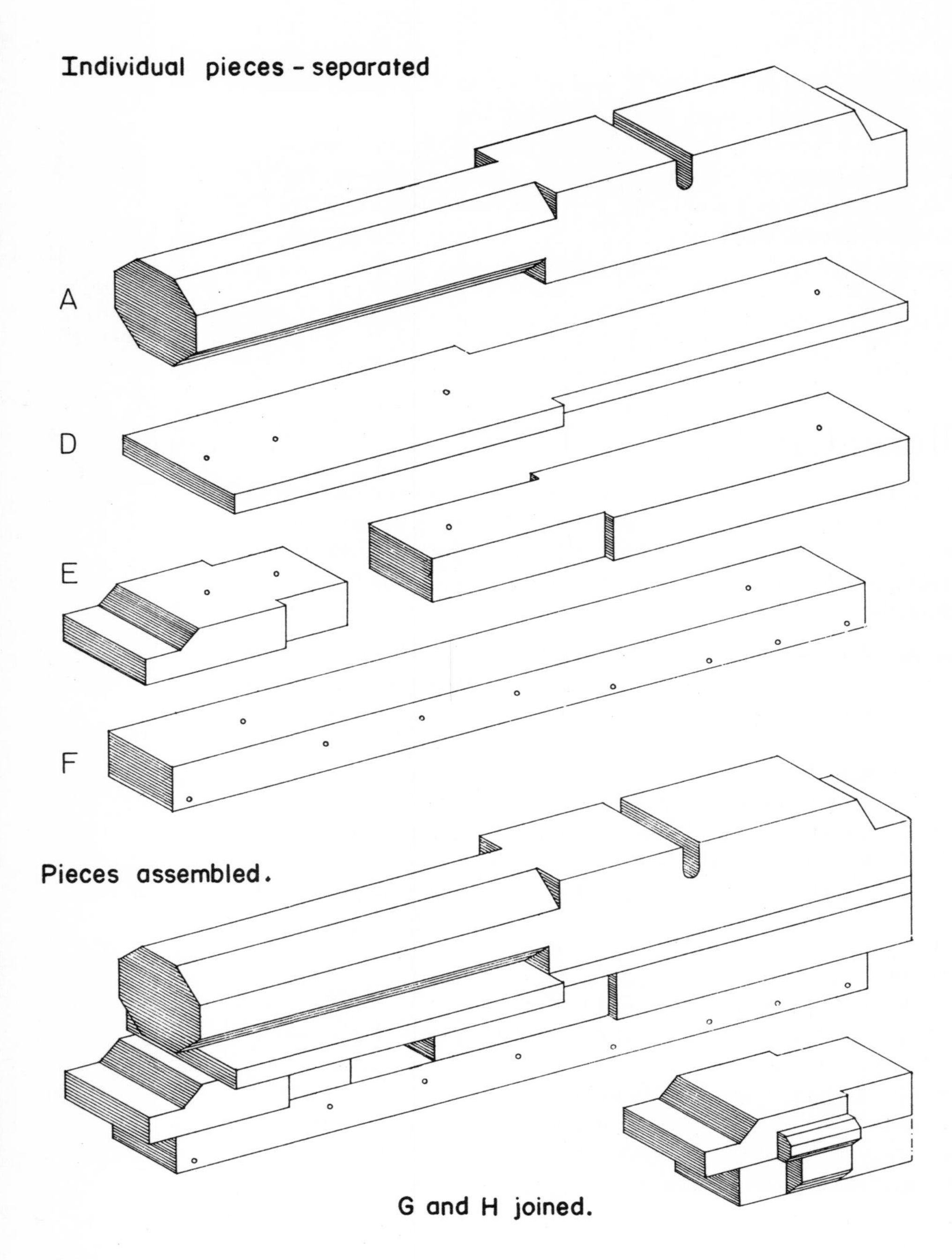

G and H joined.

Attach cylinders G and H, tank S, smokestack (made in mitre box from a piece of waste wood), shock absorbers, lights, etc.

Wheels: Bore wheels and screw them into place. If the thickness of the small wheels is greater than the 3/16″ allowed in the space between the base piece F, and side pieces B and C, the 3/16″ must be sawed off B and C's width to make room for them.

Piece can be painted with plastic paint.

Pullman Car

This is built like a strong box to which the wheel base and car sides are fastened. The sides are attached to the outside edge of the bottom while the platform pieces are set in behind the sides, and are flush with the bottom. The roof piece finishes the box and strengthens the sides and ends. The length of the cars can vary at the side lengths as desired.

Materials Base and roof: 3/4″ x 5″ x 17 1/4″ (1″ x 6″ stock). Double the length with 3 1/2″ stock.
Sides, ends, and steps: 3/8″ x 6″ x 13 3/8″ (8″ stock). Double the length with 3 1/2″ stock.
Wheel base: 1″ x 2″ x 7 1/8″ (1 1/4″ x 2 1/2″ stock)
3/16″ plywood for eight 1 1/4″ wheels
Screws: 3/4″ No. 6 roundhead; 1 1/2″ No. 6 flathead
Brads: 3/4″ 18 ga.; 7/8″ 17 ga.; and 1 1/4″ 16 ga.
Thumbtacks for shock absorbers, eyelets for wheels, and upholstery nails for ventilator.

Procedure

Base and roof: Divide the wood into a 2″ wide piece for the base, and a 3″ wide piece for the roof. (Shortening pieces to desired length can wait until the wagon is assembled.)

Saw slanted edges of roof (from a point 3/8″ in on side, to 5/8″ in at top). The length of the wood can be used as a prop in sawing.

Sides, etc.: Draw outline, following plan. Saw off the small piece F for bottom reinforcement and then divide the rest for the two side pieces.

PULLMAN CAR

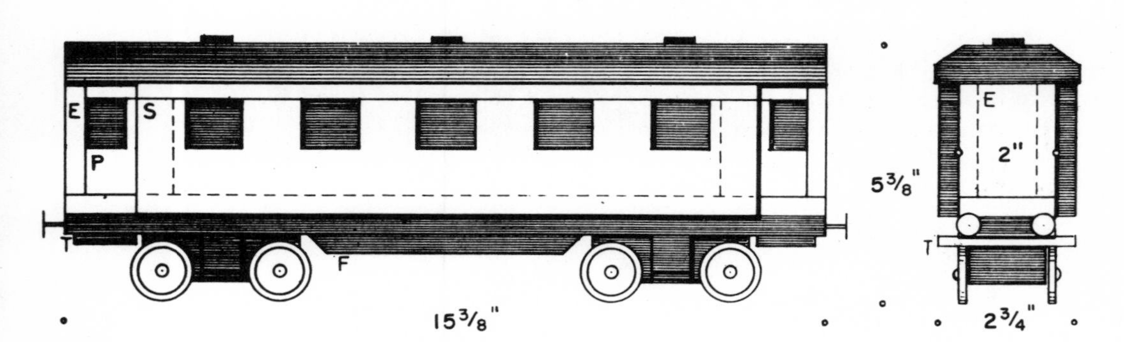

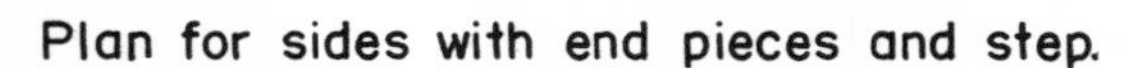
Plan for sides with end pieces and step.

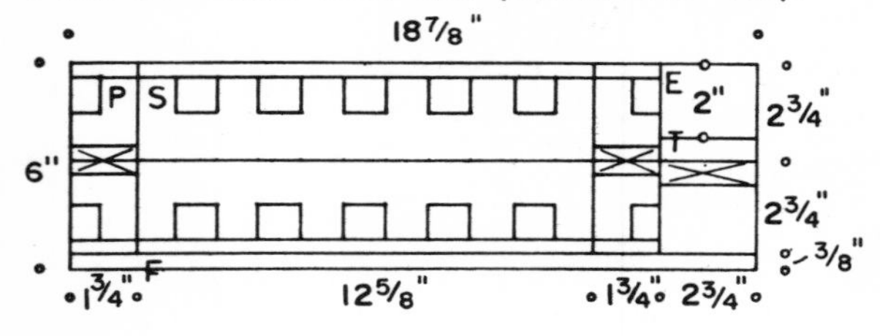

Part of side

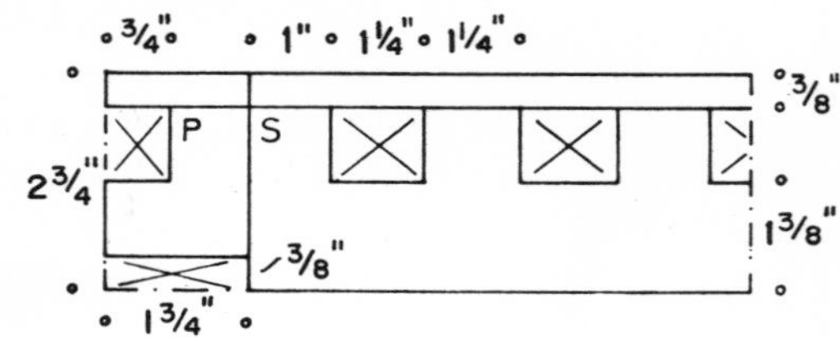

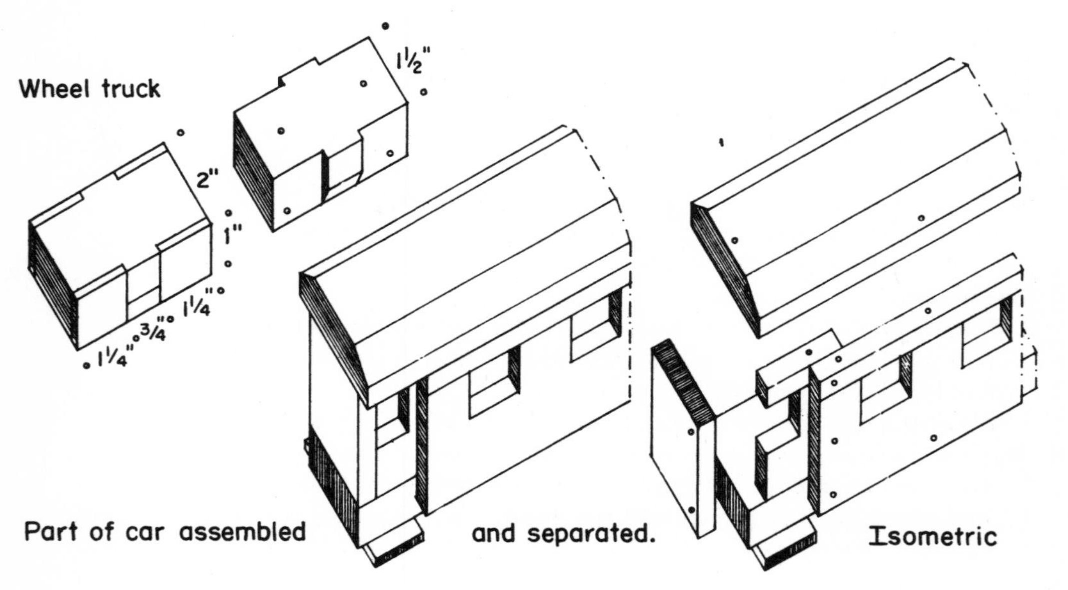

Part of car assembled and separated. Isometric

Saw off end pieces E, divide car step T, lengthwise, to half-thickness and saw it from platform piece P. (Trimming height of end piece can wait until the car is assembled.

Draw outline of sides. Saw off the piece over the windows, saw the vertical lines, then chip away the extra wood along the perpendicular line with a chisel. Nail the sawed off piece back into place over the windows.

Cut the platform pieces to the correct height and saw them away from the side pieces. Fasten them inside the side pieces so that the combined length, together with end pieces, is even with the base.

Assembly: Nail sides to car base. Nail end pieces to ends of platform sections and trim them in height to fit flush with sides.

Nail roof to sides and ends.

Wheel base, etc.: Draw outline for wheel base and saw it out. Mark position of wheels and assembly screws. Screw wheel base into place.

Make car steps and reinforcement piece and set them in place under base.

Add wheels, shock absorbers, and ventilators.

Painting: Wheel section and car base, up to the sides; roof and interior of the car should all be painted black, with the trim painted in a color.

RIFLE

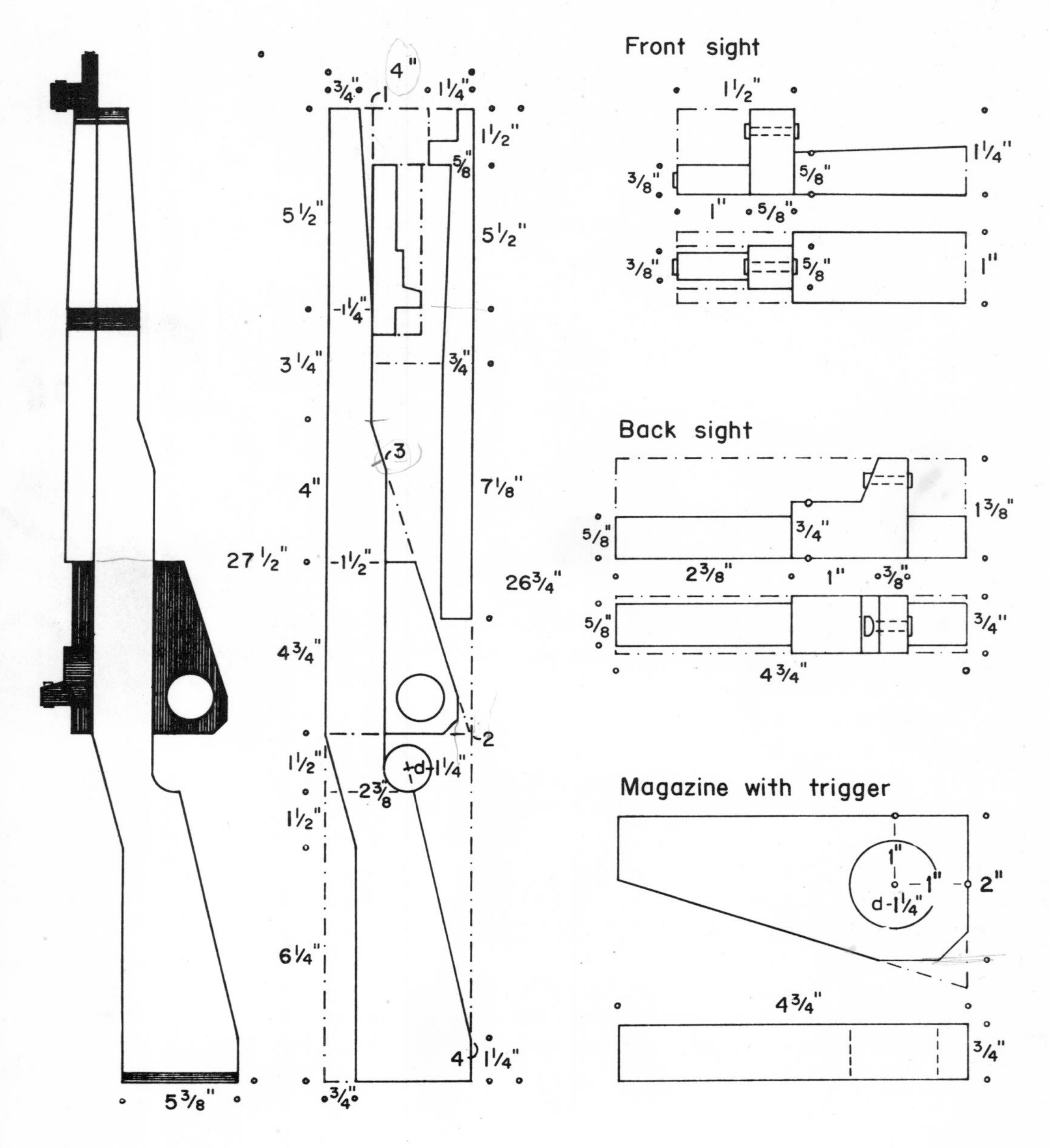

Rifle

The rifle is made in several pieces and assembled with screws and brads.

Materials Wood: 1″ x 4″ x 27½″ (1¼″ x 5″ stock)
Screws: 2″ No. 8; 1½″ No. 6 flathead
Brads: ⅞″ 17 ga.
Eyelets for sighting holes and barrel.

Procedure

Stock, with magazine and trigger hole: Draw measurements on narrow edge of wood and square them. Continue measurements onto broad surface, square, and draw outline.

Bore hole at small part of stock and trigger hole.

Saw stock in the following order:

While the stock is still undivided, the magazine with trigger hole; the barrel with front sight, lock, and back sight, must be made narrower.

Magazine: Saw 3/16″ off one side of the magazine using the bottom piece of waste wood as a prop. When the right thickness is attained, the waste piece can be sawed away.

Barrel with front sight: Make measurements on narrow edge, square, and measure onto broad surface.

Draw outline and saw out.

Making front sight and barrel point: first make the sight, follow with the barrel thickness then the barrel length. Bore a hole to make the sight.

Lock with back sight: Cut a block of wood 3/4″ x 1 3/8″ x 4 3/4″. Put measurements on underside, square, draw on measurements. Draw outline and saw. Saw the proper thickness before and after the sight, now bore a hole for the sight so that it fits the eyelet.

Painting: The shaft can be colored with wood stain and the "metal" parts can be painted steel gray with plastic paint. It is easier to paint the barrel rings if they have been indicated by saw marks.

Assembly: After painting, eyelets should be put into the holes for the sights and to simulate the barrel bores.

Fasten the barrel to the shaft from underneath, with two screws. Fasten magazine with two screws from the top, and the back sight with a pair of brads.

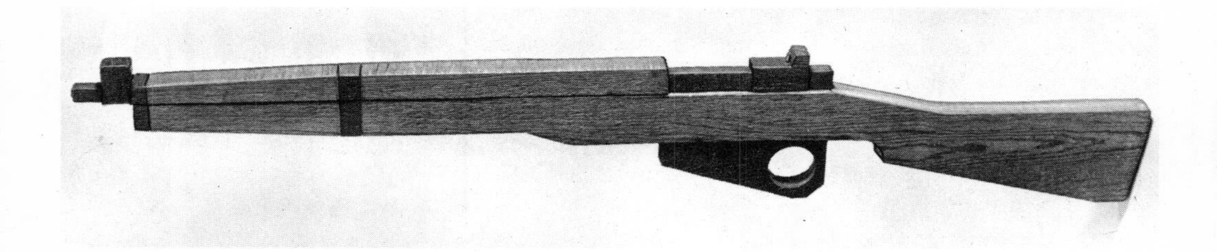

Automatic Pistol

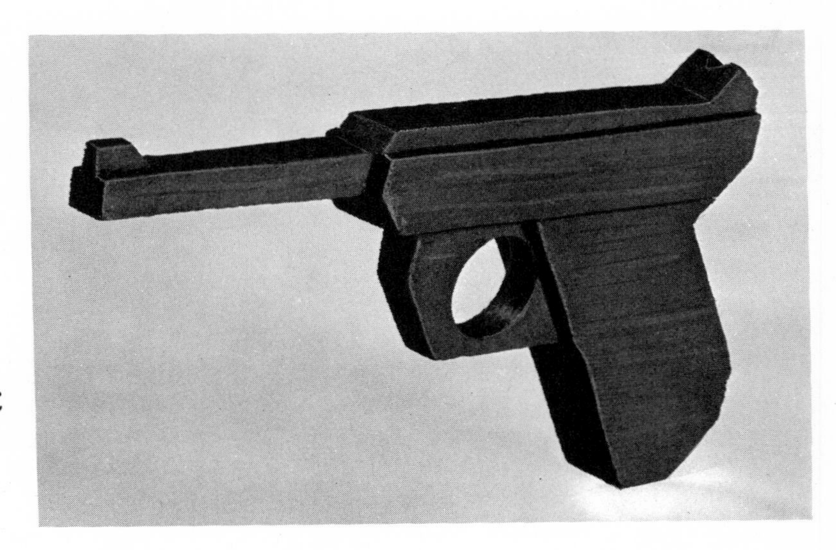

The pistol is made in three pieces and assembled with screws and brads.

Materials Wood: $\frac{3}{4}$" x 5" x $8\frac{3}{4}$" (1 x 6" stock)
Screws: $1\frac{1}{4}$" No. 6 flathead
Brads: $\frac{7}{8}$" 17 ga.
Upholstery nails, and eyelets.

Procedure

Cut the wood to a width of $4\frac{3}{8}$" and a length of 8".

Make measurements on the narrow edge, square, and draw outline on broad surface using a ruler. (See drawing page 88.)

Bore trigger hole.

As the barrel, trigger piece, and top piece must be narrower than the chamber, the pistol must be sawed apart above and below the chamber. It will be easier to begin by following the cuts in order, from 1 to 6.

When the outline of the individual pieces has been made, (back of stock is done after pistol is assembled) saw 3/16" off each side of trigger and barrel, and 3/16" off one side of top piece. Saw front sight and notch.

Assemble pistol with a $1\frac{1}{4}$" No. 6 screw from chamber down into stock under the top covering piece, and with a brad through trigger hole, up into chamber. Nail on the top piece and paint pistol with steel gray plastic paint.

Eyelets and upholstery nails make convincing barrel bore holes, safety catch, etc.

AUTOMATIC PISTOL

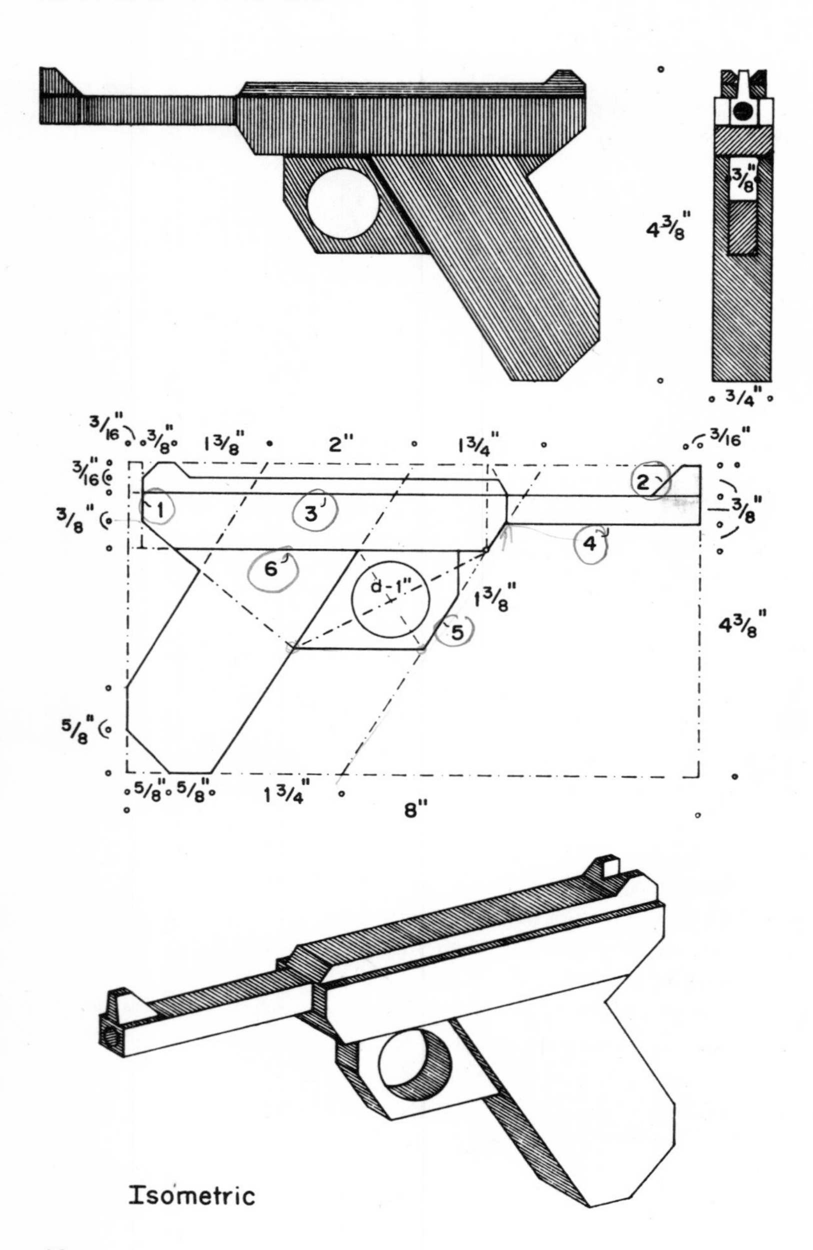

Isometric

5

3/8 = 1

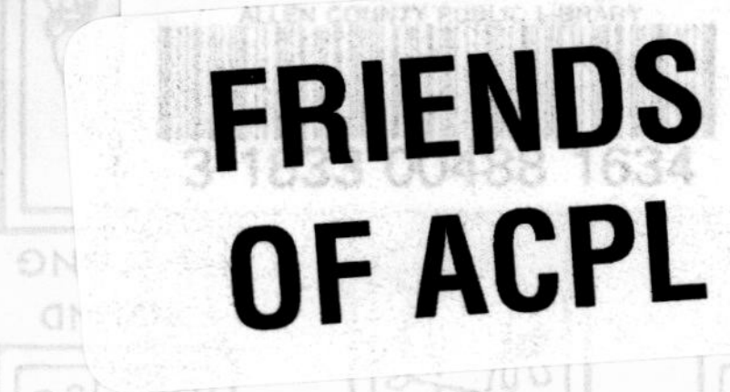